GOLF: THE UNTAPPED MARKET

GOLF: THE UNTAPPED MARKET

WHY THE PROS ARE FAILING TO GROW THE GAME

Chuck Thompson

ISBN-13: 9780692862261
ISBN-10: 0692862269
Library of Congress Control Number: 2017904173
Chuck Thompson, Jacksonville, Florida

I dedicate this book to my amazing wife, Zarita "Cherry" Thompson, and my four children, Chaz, Christian, Coley, and Azha. I am truly blessed with two angels and three champions. It is because of their sacrifices and support that I am able to realize my dream of making a difference in the world by helping others. Cherry has devoted her life to me and our children, giving us the joy of being members of a loving, happy family. She is just as proud of her titles of nurturer, wife, and mother as I am of mine as father, husband, and founder of MMC®. Together, we have found balance.

Cherry, I am not worthy of you, but I am eternally grateful for your love, and I am honored to be your husband; I know I married up. Thank you for everything, but most of all, thank you for saying yes. I love you, baby.

Revolutionize: To change something radically—to cause a radical change in something such as a method or approach.
—Encarta Dictionary

CONTENTS

INTRODUCTION

I n this book, I share my experiences of working in the golf industry, acquiring golfers, increasing revenue, and solidifying golfer loyalty. I engineered a marketing campaign that revolutionized the health-club industry and is now revolutionizing the golf industry.

Since the inception of my company, MMC® (Mulligan Marketing Concepts®), in 1991, my team and I have worked with more than seven hundred membership-based businesses and raised more than half a billion dollars in revenue for our clients while tapping into new segments, bringing affordable health and fitness as well as golf to everyone in America. In total I have been directly responsible for selling more than one million memberships and tens of millions of memberships indirectly over my thirty-five-year career. My marketing concept of using a "lost leader" (rather than the traditional "loss-leader" concept), partnered with a lower barrier to entry by redirecting the revenue stream and tapping into a new segment of consumers, is changing the golf industry forever.

MMC® profiles consumers for golf courses based on their buying patterns and spending habits. My team looks for consumers who have purchased within the golf categories and then prequalifies them through a criteria-based formula. My goal is simple: focus on identifying, engaging, and locking up long-term relationships with untapped segments—casual and nongolfers—to grow the game.

In the 1990s, golf courses were popping up on every corner, just like Starbucks coffee shops. By the turn of the century, there was too much inventory (supply) and not enough golfers (demand) to support all the new courses. The so-called experts were throwing up their hands in bewilderment while I rolled up my sleeves. In this book, I will show you how I am revolutionizing the industry through my professional sales and marketing systems and reveal the secrets you need so that you too can make your mark with your golf product or service.

Golf courses need new golfers to grow their businesses, but there are not enough core and avid golfers to sustain the more than fifteen thousand courses. I designed my no-risk self-funding campaign to target consumers who are interested in golf but have yet to be engaged—a demographic completely ignored by the golf industry.

Anyone in the golf industry, whether he or she is a course owner, manager, golf pro, sales representative, developer, marketer, retailer, merchandiser, entrepreneur, or someone in any number of other occupations, will find my research, experience and teachings useful. With my help, you will learn how to successfully sell and promote any golf product or service in any economic climate.

If you are a member of a golf course, are thinking about joining a golf course, or are wanting to pick up the game but have never been able to commit to and stick with it, you need to read this book because I teach the psychological triggers that all golf pros and instructors use (or should use) to motivate people to take action today!

As a golfer reading this book, you will learn the ins and outs of the golf industry, acquire the knowledge to get enormous discounts on memberships and green fees, and save yourself thousands of dollars by avoiding inflated dues and fees. If you are a golf pro, you will learn all the psychological triggers necessary to motivate and encourage your clients; a step-by-step system to uncover your golfers' and prospects' fears, goals, and unmet needs; and the very best professional sales system to lock up new relationships and sell more lessons, outings, clinics, and so on. As an entrepreneur, you'll learn how to package, market, and professionally sell any golf product or service; as an employee, you'll learn how to make yourself indispensable and garner job security for life; and as an owner, you'll learn how to grow your business beyond your wildest imagination and put worry and fear in the past, where they belong.

In addition, I also share my opinion on the antiquated paradigms, people, and procedures that are killing the industry today. There is something in this book for everyone because I take you on an educational journey, using my thirty-five-year career as a guide; show you how I am revolutionizing the golf industry; and give you the tools to penetrate new markets, engage golfers, and thrive in the greatest industry of all—golf. Enjoy the journey.

Wishing you good health and prosperity,

Chuck Thompson

PS: Please take a few minutes to write a review for my book, and post it on as many websites and platforms as possible with a direct link to where your friends and followers can buy Golf: The Untapped Market—Why the Pros Are Failing to Grow the Game. Also, be sure to register with my company and personal websites—www.mmctoday.com, www.golfmarketingmmc.com, and www.chuckthompson.guru (not dot com)—for freebies and updates. If you wish to contact us at MMC®, you may call 904-217-3762, call toll free 877-620-8135, or e-mail me at chuck@mmc-today.com. For comments or any other correspondence, please use my personal address at chuck@chuckthompson.guru (not dot com). Thank you, and enjoy the book.

CHAPTER 1

THE EXPLOSION AND THE CRASH

The 1990s may have been the heyday for golf courses, but by 2003, many golf courses had become ghost towns and were going bankrupt fast. Payrolls, property taxes, chemical bills, and water bills all started piling up, and soon the devastation overwhelmed owners. People were blaming the economic climate, the millennials, and even Tiger Woods. Not only were golf courses sinking faster than one of Tiger's putts, but also the downturn forced many major retailers to get out of the business completely. It was and still is bad. Pros and managers are losing their jobs, and owners are losing their courses as well as their identities as business leaders in their communities.

In 2006 MMC® entered the golf industry with a revolutionary marketing concept that would soon change the industry's way of acquiring new golfers. MMC®'s mission statement is this: Penetrate new segments of consumers using a criteria-based profile, make golf affordable by lowering the barrier-to-entry while maximizing the course's earning potential, redirect the revenue stream from the point-of-sale to the profit centers—which will ensure the business sustainable growth through committed long-term relationships with hundreds, if not thousands, of consumers (not just core and avid golfers)—and do so with dignity and integrity.

As an outsider, it is easier for me to look at the problem objectively because I am not looking through rose-colored glasses nor are my thoughts about growing the game hindered by decades of conditioning on the old golf-business model. Most people in the golf industry have this antiquated paradigm of how a golf course should be run, which is why they are running their businesses into the ground. Their industry is entrenched in their grandfathers' way of doing business. Everyone is trying to change the game when all that needs to change is the thinking.

Owners are relying on their golf pros and managers to grow their businesses when the industry is facing mass exodus as never before. In the past, golf courses didn't need to be proficient in marketing, research, demographics, psychology, professional sales, social sciences, economics, history, social media, and consumer profiling; golf courses were the original Field of Dreams: if you build a beautiful facility with all the bells and whistles, golfers will come. Golf pros are trained in PR, operations, and the game but have very little education, if any, in marketing and professional sales. Nevertheless, they are unfairly saddled with the task of saving the business. In the past, most golf courses never really had to be creative in marketing and mindlessly followed what other golf courses did as long as they weren't too far outside the box. Everyone in the golf industry was talking about growing the game, but no one had a clue as to how. Such talk was mere empty rhetoric. The biggest challenges are not the economic climate, millennials, or even Tiger; they are ego, fear, and outdated thinking.

Everyone is listening to the egomaniacs who have no stake in the business or skin in the game, preaching, "We must stick to our old way of doing business. We are special because we are golfers. Don't give golf away, and don't leave money on the table," which is code for "We are scared to death to change because we may make things worse and are desperately afraid of losing our jobs." Being afraid of changing your way of doing business is a little like being a battered spouse or partner and staying in the abusive relationship knowing full well it's only going to get worse. Sometimes people stay in very unhealthy relationships because they are afraid of the unknown. They know if they stay they are sure to get abused and experience even more pain, but they are more afraid that the unknown may be worse. They start to rationalize that things *aren't that bad*; they say to themselves, I can handle this, but things outside may be too much for me to handle, so I better stay with the status quo. The sad reality is 99 percent of the time, the lives of those people who do leave the unhealthy relationship are far better when they leave.

Some owners are taking the beating of their lives but still hang on to the old ways.

But fear is only part of the problem. A large part of the problem is the people with an elitist attitude spreading false narratives and self-serving propaganda who have kept the industry from growing over the years. While conducting focus groups during our research on casual golfers who left the game after playing only a few times, we discovered their number-one reason for leaving was because they didn't feel welcome.

The golf industry exploded in the 1990s, catering to three generations of golfers. Little did people know that Tiger Woods would be both a blessing and a curse to the game. During this decade, golf courses began to pop up everywhere, and new golfers were passing through the floodgates the Woods era had opened. Everybody and their brother were out on the course to take up the game that had been mastered by the great Tiger Woods. Developers and farmers were cashing in on the explosion. By the turn of the century, most of these enthusiastic players were long gone because they were hit with the reality of the game. Golf is an expensive sport and takes much time, study, practice, and money. Golf clubs, shoes, clothing, gas, food, green fees, cart fees, range fees, lessons, and so on added up, and soon the game became less attractive.

In 2008, the golf industry was hit with the perfect storm. In the 1990s, the baby boomers were in their peak spending years, which led to the golf industry having a huge influx of golfers—far more than ever before—because there were more baby boomers than members of any prior generation. Tiger also burst on the scene in the 1990s, which triggered an outpouring of first-time golfers who created a demand for more product. Developers went crazy building golf courses, and soon there were five to ten properties in any given market. Money was flowing like whiskey, and everyone was getting drunk on the easy instant success. As the turn of the century rolled around, the baby boomers' peak spending cycle ended, Tiger's fan club realized watching golf was more within their budget than playing it, and courses started losing some of their most dedicated core golfers to death; that is, the hero generation was starting to die off. Thus these factors, coupled with the aggressive development of golf courses, created the perfect storm that engulfed the industry. In 2003, the industry started noticing the drop-off in rounds, and in 2008, the fifth wave of the storm hit, that is, the recession. The housing bubble bursting, the baby boomers tightening their purse strings, the hero generation dying off, the Tiger wannabes leaving the game, and the onslaught of new courses were a tsunami the industry wasn't prepared for.

In chapter 8, I will explain the demographic and economic facts so that you can better understand how the baby boomers played such a significant role in this crash and how the millennials will be the generation to return the golf industry to its heyday. For now, all that is important is that you understand once the baby boomer generation started preparing for their retirement, they cut spending drastically, which had an enormous impact on the golf industry as well as the US economy and will continue to play a role until the millennials fill the void. By now (2017), the last rush of big spenders have retired and have started putting their money into safe low-to no-risk investments in preparation for their golden years. This is why the golf course industry has not seen a significant upturn in business since the decline (which really started in 2003), even though most economists say the economy is getting better, a statement I strongly disagree with. It is my belief that some golf courses will struggle (even more than in 2008) for the next decade because there is no other generation that can possibly fill this enormous void in spending over the next decade since the largest generation (premillennial) in history is retired or dying. Even if I am wrong, the millennials are the generation that courses are going to have to engage and lock up relationships with, and they are the most difficult consumers to date. The millennials won't start hitting their peak spending cycle for another decade, and the generations that came between the baby boomers and millennials can't fill that vacuum because the baby boomers (a.k.a. the "Me Generation") had far fewer children than previous generations, which means far less spending.

By 2008, rounds and revenue had already started to dwindle for most golf courses. Green fees started tanking, which has given rise to third-party tee-time vendors and discounted golf. Only the courses with deep pockets (or those who have partnered with MMC®) are surviving, and although they are feeling the pain as well, it is against their nature to let anyone know. Most high-end, ultraexclusive facilities will weather a storm because they have the resources. Eighty percent of the members of high-end golf courses are just as cash poor as you and I; however, it is the 20 percent of the members still doing well who would never let their image or the prestige of the club be tarnished by lowering membership dues or green fees. This is a healthy approach to maintaining the brand of the club if you have the needed funds or if your equity members are willing to foot the bill by covering the lost revenue.

The problem with this approach is that most golfers in the middle classes are being hit hard by the economy, and they either can't or are not willing to pick up the slack, forcing many midlevel courses to go semiprivate and abandon their private-club status. However, I believe this has turned out to be a good thing. Many course owners think of membership as a necessary evil. Every club has a few members who feel a sense of entitlement. They associate their self-worth with being members of such-and-such club. It makes them feel important (which is a core emotional need we all have but satisfy in different ways) and leads them to believe their memberships somehow give them the same rights as owners. So when some of these private clubs became semiprivate, the owners and staff enjoyed a bit of fresh air in dealing with golfers who were grateful to play the course and didn't complain about every little thing.

The challenge I have with this ill-conceived perception of not operating as a member-based club/course is the 80/20 rule. Eighty percent of members will be humble, grateful, respectful, and loyal; it is only 20 percent who will be a pain in the behind. This 20 percent is unavoidable. Whether they are members or guests, you can't change the 80/20 rule because it is a rule of nature. Loyalty programs are extremely important in all businesses, which is why every industry from the airlines to your local sandwich shop has a membership or loyalty program. I firmly believe going semiprivate can be a good thing because now more golfers can visit the course, which gives the staff the opportunity to engage them and lock up more relationships. There is always an upside to every situation, no matter how bad it seems at the time; it is up to all of us to find out what the upside is.

To combat the loss of rounds and revenue many courses, including some private, public, municipals, and nine holes, are dropping their pants with third-party tee-time vendors and daily deals. Everyone is struggling to find a way to stay afloat. The industry has never seen anything like this and, therefore, has no frame of reference to learn from and no road map to follow. All the experts are preaching from their soapboxes to just batten down the hatches and weather the storm, but that is easy for them to say because they aren't the ones drowning in debt, mowing with broken-down equipment, swimming in unpaid chemical bills, having panic attacks over back taxes, and sweating over the payroll each week. Either they have the resources or they have no skin in the game, but in no way can they relate to the majority of owners. Some of the loudest rhetoric comes from those who work for organizations that depend on golf-course owners' approval and feel they must say what they think owners want to hear because their livelihoods depend on it. Or maybe they are just some of the few who are making it and don't want their competitors making any waves in their markets. The one thing I know for sure is that they are not coming from a position of growing the game or saving the golf industry. Instead, these evangelists are preaching a self-serving gospel. Some experts even declare that this downturn is just a way of thinning out the herd. What they are really saying is that this is a great way to get rid of the competition.

The storm has made it easy for unscrupulous third-party tee-time vendors to take over courses' tee-sheets with claims of bringing more golfers and increasing revenue through more rounds, but all they bring are discounted green fees; moreover, some of these vendors keep the largest portion of what is left of the deeply discounted cart and green fees. This is a terrible option for courses because they lose complete control of their business. Golfers become conditioned to looking online for the cheapest deal of the day, making it almost impossible to lock them up in long-term relationships. This kind of customer is a one and done who offers no residual income for the course whatsoever. In addition to prostituting courses' cart and green fees while devaluing their brand, these vendors control the courses' e-mail lists, which they then mass market for their other clients' courses within the same market. Courses are dying because their core golfers are leaving their home course for discounted tee-times, and these companies prey on course owners like vultures, hovering above just waiting to go in for the kill.

E-marketing companies have also burst onto the scene, trying to brainwash course owners into thinking that the only way to make an impact is via digital marketing, also called e-marketing or cybermarketing. These companies are on the right track but are far from realizing their claims. E-marketing is the future, and millennials are the next generation to fill the vacuum in the industry as a whole, but neither millennials nor digital marketing will play the leading role in the recovery today. About a decade from now, millennials will get into their peak spending years, and digital marketing will become one of the top-three platforms. If you have your lists of followers, subscribers, friends, and so on, you will have the tools necessary to successfully market your course to certain demographics, but today there are still thousands of golf courses out there that haven't yet computerized their business operations.

Then you have the really special entrepreneurs who believe it is the game itself that needs to be changed. They pitch ideas like making the holes bigger so the game is easier or going back to the very original golf-course model, which was a twelve-hole round, as well as numerous other ideas on what I call "gimmick golf." Americans, golf enthusiasts or not, only think of golf as either eighteen or nine holes—not something in between. The game of golf is perfect just the way it is. The only thing that needs to be changed is the antiquated paradigms of the business. If you have enough money to support your course for the next ten years, then you don't have a thing to be concerned with because golf will come back and come back strong. But if you are one of those courses that are struggling, you need to be proactive. Don't be hypnotized into thinking that there are fewer golfers or too many golf courses in a given market; that the only way to engage the millennial is through digital marketing; that you must change the game; that you must let another company control your e-mail lists and tee-sheets; that if you offer something other than the norm, you'll be giving golf away; or believing any of the other BS narratives that some experts are peddling.

By misdiagnosing the problem, we will never be able to fix it. If a doctor misdiagnoses an ailment and prescribes the wrong medicine, the patient will more than likely get worse or even die. The same goes for the golf industry. If owners keep listening to the narratives being shaped by some of the industry "experts," their businesses will continue suffering and may even die.

Most markets can easily support numerous golf courses. Of course, this is a generic statement because everything is determined by numbers, and the surrounding demographics and population size will always dictate the number of courses a particular market will support. I can already hear some pros, managers, and owners screaming now, "There are twenty golf courses in my market!" Yes, I am well aware of markets like that, but the average golf course's pull from a local market is within about a thirty-mile radius. So although there may be twenty courses in your market, they are not targeting your entire market because that is a geographical improbability (unless the courses are all next door to one another), even if they are identical in product and service. The exception to the previous statement is if your golfers have to drive right past your competitors to get to your course. In that case, you better hone your marketing skills or pick up the phone and call MMC® right now.

The key to thriving in these difficult times is to grow the game by penetrating new segments of consumers. Just like there are multiple generations that must be targeted, there are different (four) types of golfers as well: core golfers, avid golfers, casual golfers, and nongolfers (i.e., golfers who have an interest in the game but have played only a handful of times in their lives, if ever). Unfortunately, the industry "experts" think of golfers only as a single group—golfers. It is this ignorance that has made it difficult for most courses to bounce back. Every community is filled with golfers who fit into one of the four segments. I am going to give you a quick overview of each, and throughout this book, I will go into detail on how to identify, engage, and lock up relationships with each segment.

There Are Four Types of Golfers

Core golfers: Core golfers are those who play at least fifty to one hundred rounds per year. Most core golfers have built relationships with other golfers/members over a period of many years and tend to stay loyal to their home courses, that is, unless their rates go up and leave golfers feeling as if they can't beat the system by playing enough rounds per year/season to justify the cost.

Core golfers play the most and spend the least. Core golfers break out the calculator and run the numbers; if they can beat the system, they join the club, but if they can't, they don't join. Core golfers don't spend a great deal of money at their home courses. They don't spend money on range balls; they chip and putt, because it's free. Core golfers don't buy logo balls, logo caps, or logo golf shirts. They don't buy clubs, shoes, gloves, or sleeves of balls from the pro shop either, because they know every discount golf outlet in town where they can buy merchandise for half the cost. Core golfers don't spend on food and beverage at the course; they bring bagged sandwiches and keep six-packs chilled in the trunks of their cars. Core golfers don't go out of the way to promote the course, because they don't want to have to wait a couple extra minutes to tee off or set tee times in advance. Core golfers are saving every penny they have to play one more round of golf. This group is addicted to the game and in most cases is on a fixed budget.

Avid golfers: Avid golfers are those who play twenty-five to fifty rounds in a year/season. These golfers are noncommitted and will play their rounds wherever they get the best deal on green fees, which means they will divide their rounds, and therefore their revenue, over several courses. This group of golfers loves the Internet and gives its "loyalty" to the deal of the day. Avid golfers don't spend money on range balls; they chip and putt, because it's free. Avid golfers don't buy logo balls, logo caps, or logo golf shirts. They don't buy clubs, shoes, gloves, or sleeves of balls from the pro shop, because they know every discount golf outlet in town where they can buy merchandise for half the cost. Avid golfers spend very little, if anything at all, on food and beverage at the course; they stop and get fast food on the way to the course. They may buy hot dogs and beer, but that's about all they will spend in the snack bar. Avid golfers don't go out of the way to promote a course. They promote the "deal of the day" and the website or company who gave them that deal; the course's name is only briefly mentioned when giving directions.

Avid and core golfers know the ins and outs of spending the least amount of money while getting the most value. Avid golfers are those who want all the same prime tee-times (Saturday and Sunday mornings) as core golfers, and they will do everything they can to beat the system.

Casual golfers: Casual golfers are consumers who play eight to twelve rounds in a year. These golfers on average play where their buddies play and have very little knowledge about the ins and outs of the golf business or Internet deals on green fees. Casual golfers are the future of the golf industry. These consumers should be the focus of every golf course, retailer, golf professional, and so on. Let me ask you a quick question: When did you spend the most money on golf? I bet your answer is when you first took up the game. Casual golfers play the least and spend the most. Casual golfers don't break out the calculator and run the numbers, don't go online to find the best deals, don't try to beat the system, and don't know the system. Casual golfers spend money on range balls, and they practice. Casual golfers impulsively buy a course's logo balls, logo caps, and logo golf shirts. They buy clubs, shoes, gloves, or sleeves of balls from the pro shop because they don't know any of the discount golf outlets in town. They spend on food and beverage at the course; they buy burgers, hot dogs, and steaks because they have come for the experience and want to enjoy the day as well as the amenities offered. Casual golfers drink at the bar and buy beer from the cart girl. They go out of the way to promote the course because the day they spent there was the best time they had all month; they tell their friends, coworkers, and anyone else who will listen. Casual golfers aren't saving every penny they have to play one more round of golf like core and avid golfers do; they spend like one-day millionaires because they golf only a few times a year. This group is consumers, and in most cases (if profiled correctly), they have disposable income.

Nongolfers: Nongolfers are those who have shown an interest in the game through their buying habits—a few rounds, equipment purchases, apparel purchases, subscriptions, and so on. These golfers play less than eight rounds a year, and some have never played a single round in their lives. They have to be identified through a consumer profile and are far more difficult to engage, but once they are, they move easily into the casual golfer segment. I have spent more than the past fifteen years developing this consumer profile to specifically address the challenges of growing the game by penetrating untapped segments.

Course owners need to cultivate relationships with casual golfers and nongolfers (consumers), who will be more apt to spend in their profit centers—for example, food and beverage, the range, and the pro shop—because they are consumers who are golfing for the experience, and they want to enjoy it to the fullest. Since this segment rarely golfs, they will spend freely. Also, casual and nongolfers are more receptive to playing during slow times and slow seasons.

I always hear about market share, but I believe in market domination. Smart course owners must think in terms of acquiring every golfer possible in their markets, no matter which category, segment, or group they fall into, because every golfer you remove from the marketplace is one more golfer (plus three, if you include his or her three buddies) your competitor can lock up a relationship with. If you are not a seasoned golf-marketing professional with an in-depth knowledge of acquiring the casual golfer and nongolfer through consumer profiling and lack the resources to acquire the pertinent data as well as the knowledge necessary to interpret that data, you will never grow the game or any golf course on a large scale.

By identifying and engaging new segments and redirecting the revenue stream of the business by repackaging the product (without discounting), you can catapult your business far ahead of your competitors. With my proven approach, you will bring in more revenue than you did in the 1990s. The glory days will come back; you just need to adjust to the times by changing your approach, not the game.

In the past eleven years, since 2006, MMC® has worked with over two hundred golf courses, sold over 250,000 golf memberships, and raised more than $50 million in up-front cash and has been directly responsible for over $150 million in back-end revenue for our clients; all during this turbulent time, when everyone else was just trying to survive—our clients thrived. In this book, you'll learn how my team and I did it and how you too can grow the game and earn millions in the golf industry by selling any golf product or service. If you own a golf course or work in the golf industry in any capacity, this book is a must read. If you just love the game of golf, you will learn about the ins and outs of the business, how to find the best deals on green fees and memberships, and the future of the golf-course industry.

I originally founded MMC® to serve the health-club industry, specializing in acquiring new members for health clubs from the difficult-to-reach and elusive market made up of deconditioned consumers (a.k.a. couch potatoes). This segment of the market was untapped by all other marketing companies and health clubs. The health-club experts focus on the health-and-fitness-conscious segment just like the golf-industry experts focus on consumers who already golf: core and avid golfers.

I founded MMC® in 1991, after having worked in the health-club industry for almost a decade in sales and marketing. I had always kept my eye on the golf industry because I could see that the bubble of the early 1990s would soon burst, knowing the baby boomers would be coming out of their peak spending years in the early twenty-first century, while developers continued building, just trying to keep up with the demand. It was crystal clear that there soon would be a demand for my expertise. In fact, I named my company Mulligan Marketing Concepts® in 1991 because I knew we would be entering the golf industry, and many courses would be needing a mulligan (a do-over)—and boy, was my prediction spot-on.

As I am writing this book, MMC® has celebrated its twenty-fifth anniversary. If you combined the total revenue generated by MMC® for our clients in the health-club industry, which is approximately $375 million plus the more than $200 million we have generated for our golf-course clients, it would tally up to $575 million brought in by our campaigns for approximately seven hundred clients (an average of $820,000 per client). To break the success of our Cash campaign down in more relatable numbers, MMC® has sold more than 750,000 memberships, which is an average of thirty thousand memberships per year; twenty-five hundred per month; and more than eighty-two memberships per day every day for the past twenty-five years. This is undeniable proof that MMC® is the world's leader in acquiring new members and growing businesses. It's not just hyperbole; it's a fact.

You learn a lot when you design and manage over seven hundred marketing campaigns. Almost everything that can happen has happened, and we have learned how to eliminate it or incorporate it to maximize the return and minimize the risk for our clients. Who would you prefer to learn from or hire to perform a delicate surgical procedure: A surgeon who has one or two surgeries under his belt or a surgeon who has more than seven hundred? It's all about the math. There are very few unknowns that arise when MMC® launches a campaign for a golf course.

Many owners, pros, and managers are too close to the problem to fix it. They are too in love with the game; too focused on their financial investment, which distorts their perceived value of the product; or they are too busy with the everyday challenges of operating a golf course to get out of their own way. The golf-course industry's ideas of marketing are antiquated, which makes their efforts impotent at best. Some pros and managers want to come in late, pull half a dozen carts, put their feet up on the desk, and watch SportsCenter reruns or ESPN. These people lack drive, energy, and intuition and don't have the slightest idea about growing the game. They are just hoping they don't lose their jobs, because having to go home and tell their wives they have to uproot their families yet again and move them across the country is a nightmare that is always playing in their minds. These people are so afraid of losing their jobs that they will do or say anything not to offend a member or disagree with the owner. This is not the mind-set you want the person who is responsible for growing or saving your business to have.

Pros love the game, but only a few love the business aspect of the game, and even fewer like the sales and marketing side of the business. Most pros want to play or teach golf and socialize with golfers, not sell memberships or market a business. Employees like these are trained in the three Ps: PR, putting golf balls, and protecting their jobs at all costs. Again, this cannot be said of all (80/20 rule) pros because I have seen numerous (the majority) pros and managers who are real go-getters and who do everything they can within their skill sets to grow the business.

Up until 2003, golf sold itself. There were only X number of courses within any given market, and each course had the play to sustain itself, so there was no need or reason for the average course to have a professional sales system or marketing strategy other than to capture the noncommitted green-fee play. The golf business has changed, and if you want to thrive (not merely survive) in the industry, you must accept certain realities; that is, you must learn a professional sales system and have an effective marketing strategy.

Golf products and services are some of the most popular inventions to be introduced to consumers, more so than in most other sports-related industries. The first thing you must do before launching a new product or service is identify your market. For example, I have written this book for four audiences: course owners, golf-industry people, golfers, and entrepreneurs. Course owners need to know how to grow their businesses, industry people need to know how to keep their jobs, golfers need to know how to get the most value for their dollar, and entrepreneurs launching new products or services need to know the entire process of taking an idea through all the stages of development and bringing it to the market.

Unfortunately for some course owners, they have to do the best with what they have. Even in the 1990s, there were several golf courses struggling with day-to-day issues that hindered them from growing organically. When most properties were feasting on the fat of the land, these courses were sucking the hind tit due to poor location and inadequate demographics. We all know the three rules in real estate—location, location, and location. But when it comes to building a golf course, sometimes the property is a family farm and moving it is, well, impossible. Owners in this situation often struggle even in the best of times, and the stagnant economic climate only worsens the situation; these owners need someone schooled in creative marketing, data, research, and professional sales systems to grow their businesses.

In 2016, I ran a campaign for a course in upstate New York in a lake vacation community that was so far off the beaten track it couldn't attract more than a handful of golfers. This course was beautiful but could never get enough play to sustain the business. The owner was constantly dipping into his pocket to cover the overhead. When he called me, he said, "Chuck, when you get lost up here, that's when you'll find the course." This course had been around for more than fifty years but had only a few golfers and even fewer guests. This course was so dead, they never had a tee-sheet.

I ran MMC®'s Cash campaign for this course when it was closed for the off-season in the middle of winter, and most of the residents were in their winter homes down in Florida. We acquired eighteen hundred golfers and raised over $320,000 in immediate cash. The owner could not believe it. He was extremely happy with the results and became one of our biggest fans. After the campaign, he said, "Chuck, when you initially told me you would acquire at least twelve hundred golfers, I thought you had been smoking something." This owner's challenge wasn't location; it was insanity. The owner had been trying the same old thing over and over and hoping for a different result. All he needed was to focus on a different segment of consumer and turn his focus away from "golfers." The population was small, but when MMC® targeted casual and non-golfers, the net was cast over a larger portion of the market and not just the traditional 8–10 percent.

This owner was a golfer who loved the game of golf and, there-fore, thought and operated his business from a golfer's perspective. Fortunately, he was smart enough to know he needed help and reached out to MMC®. Even though I love the game, I look at the golf business from a consumer's perspective and, therefore, identify with consumers' needs. The owner's focus was on acquiring golfers, and my focus was on acquiring consumers. There were more than enough consumers in his market; there just weren't enough "golfers." When the course opened in April for the season, those "consumers" spent another $400,000 in the profit centers outspending his core golfers three to one.

In the 1990s, interest in golf was outpacing the places to play, creat-ing an opportunity for developers to capitalize on the surge by providing more products—and boy, did they. Soon the tide turned, and by the late 1990s, golf courses were outpacing the demand, which made it increas-ingly more difficult for owners to survive, much less thrive. In short, there was too much inventory and not enough demand. By the early twenty-first century, golf courses were competing for golfers like never before in the history of the game. Instead of addressing the challenges head-on and truly focusing on growing interest in the game, industry people stuck to their old ways of doing business, and courses started closing their doors.

Golf is not dying, nor is there a twist to the game that can turn it around. The game is not the problem, nor is thinning out the herd the solution. The problem is the antiquated business model, inadequate marketing, lack of innovation, failure to think outside the box, stub-bornness, and sometimes-elitist attitudes. I see courses unnecessarily going under all the time, selling to developers for pennies on the dollar, and I go nuts. If owners and city officials just got out of their own way and changed their focus, they could easily save these courses and make a fortune for themselves, their investors, and their cities. The problem is that they throw their hands up in frustration after trying the same thing over and over and over without any success (duh!). This brilliant business decision is bad for the community and economy and, worst of all, puts people out of work.

There are three simple steps to success for any brick-and-mortar venture, which I call the three Ss of business: sales, service, and sanitation. Sales always come first because if you do not have golfers, then you don't have anyone to offer service to, nor do you have the revenue to hire someone to keep the place clean. Sales are the foundation of any business, but most owners and operators are unaware of the successful systems available that can make the difference between thriving and barely getting by.

This is one of the things that really concern me about municipal properties. People in positions of power don't know how to make a course produce revenue, which puts a strain on the city's budget and leaves city officials throwing up their hands and feeling forced to liquidate the real estate or turn it over to incompetent management groups. I actually spoke with an owner (lessee) who has a lease on a municipal course for $1,000 a year! This guy and his partner have absolutely no skin in the game other than some improvements they have made from the revenue the course is already generating. The city has all the risk and receives $1,000 a year for its multimillion-dollar investment—go figure. Cities need these courses to thrive and not drain the budget. The success of any city depends on attracting new businesses, which creates jobs; the new jobs bring new families who buy homes, which in turn raises tax revenue across the board. There is no better attraction to sell a company's board members on moving to your city than a beautiful golf course. Even those residents of a community who do not golf love the beauty of huge open green spaces like a golf course. This can be compared to the indoor pool, which is one of the biggest expenses in the health-club business and is used by only a few of the members, but—and this is a huge but—it is also one of the biggest draws and one of the biggest sales tools to lock up new relationships. Members love knowing it's there—whether they use it or not. The powers that be in the parks department really need to do their best to save their golf courses because they are important sales tools for any city, town, or community.

As I write this book, MMC® has just wrapped up a campaign for a municipal course in Colorado. The pro called me and asked if we could help him save his course. Within a very short time after launching the campaign, we raised almost $250,000 in immediate cash for the course (city) and brought them in more than fourteen hundred golfers. From those golfers alone, the course is projected to earn $280,000 in back-end revenue in just cart fees and food and beverage when they open for their season and an additional $280,000 each year for two more years after that. By targeting consumers instead of golfers, MMC® was able to generate more than half a million dollars in the first year, and the course is projected to raise an additional half million over the next two years.

On the other hand, had the pro not been searching for new ideas outside the norm and convinced his superiors to bring in MMC®, he could have let the property fall victim to some of the "industry experts." All a course ever has to do is change the target market from core and avid golfers (which is whom everyone else in the market is unsuccessfully targeting) to casual and nongolfers, bring MMC® in to profile, engage and acquire the casual and nongolfers, and the course will make a fortune with no downside, including no investment.

While on the subject of course development, I want to share my thoughts on the future of the golf-course business. I have been predicting and getting out ahead of trends in the health-club and, now, golf industry since the early 1980s, and I have a new prediction for the industry. It is my strong belief that first-class regulation nine-hole properties are going to become the more popular properties with millennials and future generations to come. Millennials will have far less time and patience to invest six hours (a four-hour round plus drive time and lunch) into playing a round of golf than their predecessors. The millennial golfer will be far less dedicated to the game and will have a much shorter attention span than generations past. There will always be a place for country clubs and some eighteen-hole facilities, but I feel the real money will be in owning a first-class regulation nine hole with three par 5s, four par 4s, and two par 3 holes. The par 5s are an absolute necessity because golfers love to pull out the big dogs and knock the cover off the ball, but after nine holes, they will be bored and ready to go on to the next thing, and if marketed correctly, that next hole will be the tenth hole or should I say the bar and restaurant.

I previously mentioned the new push to take golf back to twelve holes in an attempt to shorten the round to three hours. My pushback with this model is that the time shaved off the round is not enough. Golfers think of the round and forget about the drive time, prep time, BS time, time to settle bets, eating, drinking, and so on. Eighteen holes of golf is a good six- to eight-hour day. Most core and avid golfers try to get in and out, because it is all about the round, whereas to casual and non-golfers, including a few avid golfers, it is about the experience. Playing nine holes cuts a good two to three hours off the time, making a round far more attractive to the lifestyles of the new generation of consumers entering the game. Besides, twelve holes just sounds completely foreign to most golfers, even if you do call it "American golf." Nine holes, on the other hand, has already been conditioned into our psyches.

I am not saying this so that all owners will sell off nine holes. As I said, there will always be a market for eighteen-hole facilities, especially for the core golfer, but the generations that have and will come after the baby boomers are different consumers. Besides, if you already have an eighteen-hole course, it could easily be converted into two nine-hole courses when the time comes, giving your golfers an option to play one of two different courses. I also believe in a decade or so that most nine-hole courses will be able to charge just as much as an eighteen-hole course does now. This is not a hypothesis; this is a fact based on MMC® data and experience.

Most generations of the past grew up throwing a ball. Whether it was playing football, baseball, or basketball, kids went outside and threw balls—it was what we did. Even if you weren't an athlete or didn't play organized sports for your school or a community league, you still threw and caught some kind of ball in some field or for a pickup game in your neighborhood. Today, if I threw a kid a ball, there is a good chance he wouldn't catch it and an even better chance he may hurt himself trying to catch it.

Golf is a sport where older athletes can still be competitive. The sad reality is the closest some millennials get to throwing a ball is with their thumbs on a video-game controller, iPad, or mobile device. Since this generation is also secluded in their bedrooms, and they don't socialize in person, they don't miss the camaraderie of playing sports either. The great news is that millennials are getting more health conscious than the previous generations, and although the percentage of athletes is not impressive, the sheer number of them will breathe life back into the game in the next decade.

But nine-hole facilities are the future of the golf industry, not the solution for today. We need to address the current challenges facing the industry and save businesses today. Industry people need to focus their attention primarily on locking up relationships with casual and nongolfers, bring back those golfers who tried the game in the 1990s and left because they felt unwelcome or were left on their own to fend for themselves, and engage the future golfers—the millennials.

The reality is, in some cases, we have to address poor course conditions, a course coming out of bankruptcy, a course that has sold off nine holes out of desperation (not forward thinking) just to stay afloat, a change of ownership, a change of management, and so on. All these challenges can easily be overcome if you put your thinking cap on and take off the blinders so that you can see the challenge facing your business for what it really is: a challenge that needs to be addressed, overcome, and turned into a positive. Always think of problems as challenges because problems seem difficult and are usually avoided at all costs, whereas challenges are exciting and welcome creative thought.

Staffing issues is one of the challenges that has plagued the industry and proved to be an obstacle for golf courses. Being a great manager has nothing to do with having the ability to accomplish tasks better than everyone else. Whether someone is a good or great manager depends on how well he or she can assemble a team of people who know how to work to their strengths and are better in their fields than the manager is. If you need a bookkeeper, find someone who loves numbers, has an eye for detail, and likes to work alone; hire people who have the skill sets to match their positions. When you can build a team that works together seamlessly, everyone wins. Don't be afraid to hire people who can do things better than you. For example, when do you normally play your best round of golf? For me, the answer is easy: when I play someone far better than myself. Surround yourself with the best, and your business and career will surpass your wildest dreams.

I hire salespeople for sales, attorneys for legal advice, and accountants for accounting. When I hear someone say, "I wear all the hats," I think to myself, Then you are operating in a deficit. A jack-of-all-trades is a master of none. I know there are many one-man bands out there trying their best to do it all out of necessity, and I truly empathize with their situation. My tip for them is to be creative and find ways to bring professionals into their lives. One way I used to get professional help from people when their services weren't in the budget was to barter a membership(s) for the owners, employees, or family members—whatever it took to get the professional for the job. There is always a way; it is up to you to find it. Of course, in golf, rounds, range balls, outings, and function halls can all be bartered.

Sales are the backbone of everything in life, from products to relationships, and people are selling every day, whether you realize it or not. You sell your kids on putting their coats on before they go outside, you sell your girlfriend on becoming your wife, you sell the plumber on fixing the sink today and not tomorrow, you sell yourself in a job interview, you sell yourself to a group of friends, and so on. We live in a world dependent on sales skills, so why not invest the time to learn how to sell effectively?

Forget growing the game for a minute because, let's face it, most people in the golf industry can't even sell hardcore golfers who spend large portions of their day thinking about golf on products or services, much less sell consumers on the idea of taking up the sport (lifestyle). In fairness, though, industry people never had to learn professional sales until now. Basically, a golf membership sales presentation was as follows: "These are our membership fees, these are our green fees, and this is our model—take it or leave it." Club employees are taught to keep members happy at all costs. The golden rule is to not say or do anything that may upset a member. Golf courses need core members to sustain the business, but these members must understand that owners need revenue to operate the business, and most courses can't acquire enough core golfers willing to commit to a traditional membership to sustain the business and its growth. This reality is forcing most private clubs to turn semiprivate in order to bring in revenue through green-fee play, merchandise sales, increased food-and-beverage sales, and so on.

The sad reality is that core and avid golfers spend very little in their home course's profit centers. Core golfers rarely if ever hit range balls. Core golfers don't buy tees, golf bags, or golf clubs from the pro shop. It is a fact that most core golfers spend the least amount of money (unless there is a club or food minimum) at the course, yet they are the most targeted by golf courses. It is the new golfer who goes to the range once or twice a week. It is the new golfer who spends in the pro shop and impulsively buys the golf clubs and golf bag. It is the new golfer who brings in all his or her friends because he or she is so excited about being a member of the club. It is the new golfer who spends in the bar after a round and in the restaurant for lunch and sometimes dinner. It is the new golfer who attends clinics and takes lessons. In most cases, the new golfer outspends the core golfer three to one. If we know these facts, then why do most industry people focus on the core and avid golfer? The answer is plain and simple: *it is all they know.*

Golf courses are so afraid of losing even one golfer because the lost revenue has a devastating effect on the business's bottom line. Because of this, the golf pro or manager lives in fear and is enslaved by the club's members. It is impossible to grow a business in a state of fear. The good news is innovation comes from either inspiration or desperation. Some course owners who have been faced with the economic realities of owning a golf course in the twenty-first century are trying new things—some good, some bad.

Most core golfers join a specific golf course because of one of two reasons: cost or prestige. Location is important but secondary. We all have core emotional needs we must satisfy, and one of those needs is to feel important, significant, and successful, and being a member of the right club(s) fulfills this core emotional need. Most core golfers just love the game and want to play as many rounds as possible for the least amount of money, so the calculator determines a large part of their decision processes. They know they will play approximately one hundred rounds per year (season), and the math will decide where their "loyalty" goes.

The bottom line is that most golfers are looking out for themselves, and unless your members are shareholders, equity members, or certificate members, you can't let them dictate the way you run your business. With that said, you must do everything within your power and within reason to provide the very best product and customer service possible and do so with a gratitude for their patronage and loyalty. Sales, service, and sanitation (in that order) are some of the fundamental keys to successfully operating a golf course. Selling golfers on long-term loyalty programs, providing unparalleled service, and keeping the course and clubhouse (pro shop) clean and pristine whenever possible are paramount.

Members of golf courses are spoiled, and in some cases, you'll find some members to be selfish, concerned with their own needs only. They want the course to themselves and don't want to be bothered with reserving a tee-time or waiting two minutes to tee off. I salute those golfers but only if they are willing to pony up and pay more for those privileges to support the club. As these golfers want to grow their own businesses, they must realize that clubs are businesses too and must turn a profit and grow with the cost of living.

A big fear of most courses is to have slow play, and rightly so. No one wants to play a five-hour round. Because of this fear, most industry guys shy away from anything outside the box when it comes to marketing. This fear of overcrowding the course, slow play, or upsetting one or two of the core members paralyzes the business's growth. You can grow the business and still get in four-hour rounds if you target new segments of golfers and condition them at the point of sale to play during slow times and on slow days. This is a win-win for the business and the current golfers. By simply redirecting your focus, you are able to maintain and, in most cases, increase the level of service the core golfer is receiving as well as grow the business.

This issue of overcrowding is a concern I often have to address when speaking with course owners and their staff who are concerned with slow play. Since the industry has no frame of reference for maximizing tee-times, I completely understand their concern, although it is unfounded.

There is a belief in the golf industry that a course can host only as much as thirty-five thousand rounds per year (based on a thirty-week season). In fact, most people in the industry believe this is the absolute maximum number of rounds a property should host to guarantee the golfer the most valued experience. I too agree with this arbitrary number if you are wanting to project the image of "You have the course all to yourself," provided your course has the golfers willing to pay the fees necessary to support the course while providing the owners with a modest ROI, but if you are in a competitive market, I suggest you rethink that belief.

The pushback I have with the thirty-five-thousand-round model is that it has been built around only ten hours of the week—Saturdays and Sundays, 6:00 a.m.–11:00 a.m., which are the most coveted tee-times and are, therefore, treasured and guarded. Think about it: these are the only tee-times (for most golf courses) that are in high demand. The rest of the times and days, most golf courses are wide open, especially during their off-season. I know you probably have a morning men's league and a seniors' league, besides a few other leagues and outings, but most properties are offering every daily discount in the world to get golfers out on the course.

Some people in the golf industry are setting themselves and their courses up for financial suicide by the limitations of their own minds. You must shake this old, out-of-date, financially devastating paradigm and replace it with a new, empowering one. Besides, when is the course the most fun? When it's busy, of course! You have to be there anyway, so you might as well be busy doing what you love—spending your time with golfers. Don't think of increased rounds as more work for the same money. Instead, think of more rounds as more lessons, more job security, more stability for your family, and so on.

MMC® has consistently increased rounds at our partnering golf courses (well over two hundred thus far since 2006) by ten thousand to fifteen thousand rounds per year, which has, as a by-product of these increased rounds, increased annual revenue by as much as $500,000 per year. Our clients were hosting fifteen thousand to thirty thousand rounds before partnering with MMC®, so even after we complete our golfer-acquisition campaign, we still fall within the range of the industry standard of about 35,000 rounds per year and far short of the real number of almost 53,000 possible rounds that can be hosted by a course in a thirty-week season.

Here are the real numbers:

If you set your tee-times every eight minutes, that gives you seven tee-times an hour times four golfers, which equals twenty-eight golfers (giving the starter time to catch up with a grace period of four minutes an hour), and if you are open 6:00 a.m.–3:00 p.m., you have a solid nine hours of tee-times (not factoring in additional operational hours, for example, 5:30 a.m.–7:00 p.m.). Multiply nine hours times twenty-eight golfers and you get 252 rounds of golf per day (with thirty-six minutes of grace time for the starter), and this isn't even crazy busy; this is just operating at peak performance.

7 days × 252 rounds = 1,764 rounds per week

1,764 rounds × 30 weeks = 52,920 rounds

52,920 rounds – X (X = number of rounds you are currently hosting) = "____" available rounds.

I understand you want the course to be in the best shape possible and do not want it to be overplayed. But again, put your commonsense cap on for a minute, and think: Isn't it far easier to keep course conditions at their best when you are not worried about revenue? Besides, the reality is most golf courses will never get to experience the joy of 52,920 rounds (even after partnering with MMC®) in a thirty-week season. But if that were possible, there would never be any reason for concern because, just like the numbers (numbers don't lie) above prove, it is possible to host almost fifty-three thousand rounds per thirty-week season. There is data just as plausible that proves the enormous increase wouldn't last long because everyone is always most excited in the beginning, and some golfers' play will inevitably drop off over time. Stop putting the cart before the horse, quit worrying if you can handle the additional rounds, and get focused on acquiring the additional rounds.

This is not an attempt to get everyone striving to host more than fifty thousand rounds of golf, but it is an eye-opening snapshot of the possibilities for those of you not seeing an acceptable return on your investment and thinking there is no way to grow because you are at capacity. If you are hosting thirty thousand rounds and are happy with your revenue stream, then stay with thirty thousand, but if you are hosting thirty thousand rounds and are dissatisfied with your revenue stream, know there are ways to grow without diminishing the golfing experience.

The golf industry is changing from the Field of Dreams to a business propelled by marketing and sales, just like most other businesses in this world. The powers that be better start embracing professional sales and marketing with open arms, or their highbrow attitudes will kill the average course and stifle the growth of the game permanently. Unfortunately, it is some of the elitist crowd (and elitist wannabes) spreading their self-serving propaganda who are doing the most damage to the game and to the struggling golf courses.

I often run into concerns about introducing professional sales systems as well as marketing strategies geared to acquire new golfers, because finding competent staff is challenging for most owners. Most of the time, owners end up with students working part-time at the front counter just to get through school. These students just want paychecks and have little to no interest in making the golf business a career. Some owners feel their businesses are trapped in mediocrity, because their staff is just not motivated. Golf courses need presentable people, and sometimes the best-looking, backslapping, "yes, sir; yes, ma'am" people are not the go-getters owners need. I understand this dilemma well, because the health-club industry is full of good-looking people, and some are not the sharpest tools in the shed. This prompted me to address the challenge when building my golf-marketing campaigns, where I eliminated the need for professional salespeople. I designed our campaigns around the existing staff's strengths as well as their limitations. I am always looking for ways to turn lemons into lemonade. When I'm faced with challenges, I ask myself, "How can I make this work?" and "What is good about this?" Golf-course owners must do the same.

This brings me to two of the most disturbing things I first noticed in the golf industry. First, golf courses across the United States seem to have exactly the same staff, as if the staff had been cloned (i.e., they look alike; walk alike; talk alike; and, worst of all, think alike). Second, since very few industry people are educated in professional sales and marketing, "borrowing" other courses' and people's ideas, materials, marketing campaigns, and just about everything else is considered normal, which up until the turn of the century didn't have as much of a negative impact on the industry as it has today.

Golf pros are a tight-knit group, as they should be. The challenge with this brotherhood is that it can be a double-edged sword. Golf professionals are some of the most well-liked guys in any industry. In fact, they are almost similar in every way. Golf pros must be personable, friendly, well dressed, well groomed, well versed in public relations, presentable, and well spoken. By nature, they want to help one another, and as we all know, up until now they have never had to fear one another competing for the same resources, so they feel comfortable sharing their marketing successes. The challenge with this camaraderie is twofold. First, once the information has been passed from one pro to the next, it diminishes in detail, and second, the industry has changed so much (and since there is so much inventory) that now most courses are competing for some of the same resources, so the effect of the marketing gets watered down. This genuine desire to help others or themselves is contributing to the death of golf properties across America.

Here is an example: After we completed the course I previously mentioned in upstate New York, the owner was extremely happy and wanted to share the success with his friends in the industry. He had long conversations with many of his friends, but two of them who both own golf courses come to mind. He told both owners they needed to call me immediately so that they could stop feeding the businesses out of their pockets and make them profitable. The first one thought he had all the information to do it on his own from his conversations with our client, and the second called us, wanting us to run our campaign his way with his ideas. Both of these owners failed to grasp the concept of the campaign. It is only because we know how to identify, engage, and lock up relationships with untapped segments, as well as tailor, structure, and manage the campaigns, that our campaigns are so successful. Their ideas (what they have done in the past) won't work just because they know the price point MMC® used as a hook to grab the attention of casual and nongolfers for the New York course. The campaign is not designed to target core and avid golfers. Launching a campaign with only the knowledge of MMC®'s price point and using that price point to target core and avid golfers is a bad idea and could result in financial suicide. Think of it this way: if you need heart surgery, you hire the best heart surgeon you can afford. You don't hire someone who has "second-hand information" on how to repair the damage, nor do you go through with the surgery. The same goes for growing a business—you do what is necessary, and you hire professionals to do it.

Our client is a great guy, and his heart is in the right place. I know for a fact he told both of these owners they needed to call us, but it was their egos and greed that made them feel it was better to either change the way we do the campaign or do it on their own. Both ways, by the way, are recipes for financial disaster. We have been growing businesses for twenty-five years and have tried most (though not all) approaches, and if we have tried an idea that didn't work, despite all our knowledge and experience, why would an owner not use our history to guarantee his or her own success? We made the mistakes and suffered the consequences so that our clients wouldn't have to. Both of these owners were going to worsen their situations, and this was in no way our client's fault. Unknowingly, out of a desire to help, our client had given these two cowboys just enough rope to hang themselves, but he did not tell them to buy the rope, tie the noose, and jump off the horse.

One of the million things I've learned in my career is that many people know what to do, but they don't always do what they know. For example, I put a free download on my company's website (golfmarket-ingmmc.com) to teach anyone who wants to learn every step he or she needs to know about how to professionally lock up relationships with golfers. Yet most course owners, managers, and pros still do not go to the site and download this free tool, and even if they do, they fail to use this system the way it was designed to be used. This simple step-by-step provided in the download could easily triple a course's revenue overnight, and it is absolutely free, yet they don't study and learn it. And when they do use it, they skip steps or even full sections. This system has been developed over thirty-five years and proven in over seven hundred successful marketing campaigns across America, and people still don't follow it correctly. My point is I could give most people every detail of our Cash campaign, and they would still screw it up, because they would cut corners, not follow the structure, look for ways to save money, miss steps, miss deadlines, forget to inspect what they expect, not follow the action steps, not commit the necessary time, fail to pay attention to the details, lose focus, become lazy, and on and on.

I love marketing and growing businesses; this is my life's purpose and passion, not playing golf. I was introduced to the game of golf by one of the guys who worked for a health club in South Carolina, for which I was running a marketing campaign around 1990. The first time I stepped on the tee-box and looked out over the dew-covered fairways and greens, I was hooked and fell in love with the game. In the mid-1990s, I started studying the golf industry, and I realized it was going to crash and burn at the turn of the century. In 2000, I started adapting to the golf industry everything I had learned over the previous eighteen years of selling memberships and acquiring new members from untapped segments through consumer profiling and opened MMC®'s golf division in late 2005, and I launched our first Cash campaign for a golf course in southern Illinois in January 2006.

After entering the golf industry, I discovered that a large percentage of golf pros are in constant fear of losing their jobs. At first, this struck me as odd since most markets have numerous golf courses and then it dawned on me. These people have no job security because they have never been taught how to professionally market and sell their products. I had always heard and read stories about everyone in the golf business wanting to "grow the game," but some of these people didn't have any experience with growing a lemonade stand much less an industry. After they read this book, that will no longer be the case.

I am a firm believer in giving value, and since you parted with your hard-earned capital to buy this book, I want to ensure you receive enormous value. So I am going to give you the details of how I constructed this professional sales system and then you can go to our website, www.golfmarketingmmc.com, and get the free download; then you will have at your disposal my entire system, which I have been updating every year since the early 1980s. Throughout chapter 2, I will reference some of the forms pertinent to this system, but since you can get them off our site, print-ready, I don't want to take up valuable space in this book with them. I prefer to fill it with more detailed information to teach you the psychology, social sciences, and data that are the behind-the-scenes tools used to create this system so that you too can custom-design a sales system for any golf product or service you choose.

The three-S rule—sales, service, and sanitation—is a much-debated subject with regard to which S comes first (similar to the chicken or the egg) with business people (since they are all equally important). As I have stated many times, some owners, pros, and managers are delusional about the golf-course business and still believe in the Field of Dreams: if you build a beautiful facility with all the bells and whistles, golfers will come. Most people are curious by nature and love to see new things, including golf courses. But that's where the fantasy falls apart, along with most new owners' dreams. Golfers have more options today than ever before, and what's more, they have access to them on their gadgets. Most prospects don't even have to set one foot on your property to know what your business offers; most of your information is just a mouse click away. They simply go online and see everything you have to offer from the comfort of their homes. Owning a brick-and-mortar business today is tough. We need prospects to come in the door so that their senses can engage with the product. Sales is hands down the most important of the three Ss.

Sales and salespeople have gotten a bad reputation over the years because of a few bad apples, but I guarantee you this country, your state, your business, your home, and your lifestyle all have a salesperson who made it happen. Everything you love has a sale behind it. I am married with four kids aged ten through fourteen, and every day I face some of the best salesmanship I've ever seen. When my kids (especially my third son, Coley) want to go somewhere or do something, they turn on the sales charm; when my wife wants something, she knows how to get me to say yes in a second. All people are selling themselves daily, to their spouses, parents, coworkers, friends, relatives, bosses, kids, and so on. Anytime you want something or want to get your way, you are in a sales presentation.

Sales are the backbone of any business. Think about it: there is a ton of great products sitting in warehouses that has never made it to the consumer because no one effectively sold those products to the public. How many great musicians, writers, actors, inventors, and so on do you know who never made it because they didn't try (or know how) to sell themselves? On the other hand, look at the most successful people in the world, and I guarantee you they are salespeople. Steve Jobs and Bill Gates are thought of as tech guys, but those two billionaires were greater salesmen by far. Bill sold his software to IBM, and Steve sold Apple to the world.

A sale takes place when one person transfers to another person his or her enthusiasm about a product, a service, an idea, a dream, a marriage proposal, a night at a friend's house—literally anything and everything you can think of.

So if you know salespeople shape the world, and you want to shape the world, why not become the best damn salesperson ever? If you have the heart, I guarantee you that you will obtain the tools in chapter 2. I cannot stress how important it is that you learn how to sell yourself, your course, your products, and your services if you want to have any success whatsoever. So whether you are selling golf equipment, chemicals, merchandise, outings, food and beverage, events, lessons, clinics, or whatever, you will still be able to use this system. Also, if you are just a golf enthusiast, you will learn all the techniques salespeople are using when you buy a product or service, including a golf membership, which will give you the upper hand and save you thousands of dollars in membership and green fees.

Private clubs keep lowering their dues, hoping they will attract more members and increase member retention. Unfortunately, all they are doing is losing even more money because, with their current model and targeted market, they can't possibly get ahead of the attrition. A course adds ten members and loses twenty to death or economics, and the reduction in membership rates isn't deep enough to attract enough golfers to offset the reduced rates. Regrettably, this strategy devastates the business. Not only does the course still lose members, but now it is also collecting less revenue from the remaining members. Growing your business by targeting new segments and learning how to sell your product effectively is the only way to thrive!

Never forget—it is newbies and casual golfers who buy logo balls, logo caps, shirts, shorts, socks, shoes, gloves, tees, and occasionally a set of clubs from the course's pro shop when they first start playing the game. It is newbies and casual golfers who go to the range, not core or avid golfers. Newbies and casual golfers eat in the restaurant and drink in the bar. Think back to when you were a kid and your mom wanted you to take a bag lunch to school, but you wanted to fit in with your friends and buy from the cafeteria? Well, newbies and casual golfers want to fit in with the other members of the club and will spend like drunken sailors to do so. Core and avid golfers get their feeling of importance by the score on their card or from improving their handicap. Casual golfers and newbies get their feeling of significance from buying a five-dollar beer, shiny new golf balls, brand-name golf bags, clubs, clothing, and so on. The growth of the business and industry depends on knowing how to professionally sell to newbies and casual golfers.

Newbies scare some owners and scare superintendents even more. They worry these new golfers will wreak havoc on the course and/or slow up play. This challenge can easily be avoided by requiring new golfers to attend a free (or paid) seminar or clinic on the game, course etiquette, club rules and rules of the game, and so on. You can even require a written or oral exam for those who feel they do not need to attend the clinic or seminar to prove their awareness and understanding of the rules. Either way, you can explain (sell them on) the necessity by informing new golfers it is for their safety and the safety of other golfers.

In the early years of my career, after successfully growing a handful of health clubs and moving up the corporate ladder, starting in a sales position and moving up to assistant manager, manager, area director, and eventually becoming a consultant, I realized the only way I was going to make a mark on the industry, which I was destined to make, was by becoming a marketing guru. The way I saw it, marketing was just sales, but instead of selling one on one, a marketer sells to the masses. I set a goal to work with numerous clubs throughout the United States and engineer a universal marketing campaign that could be implemented in any and every health club nationwide (which I later adapted to the golf industry). It wouldn't be a cookie-cutter campaign but a universal campaign that could be tailored to the specific needs of any club yet yield similar results in any market.

You must first learn how to walk before you run though, you must have a strong foundation to build a stable home, and you must first learn how to sell a golf membership to a golfer before you can ever grow the game or a business. Think of it this way: How can you sell the game of golf to consumers who rarely if ever play, if you can't even sell a golfer who loves the game a membership, annual pass, hot dog, beer, bucket of balls, persuade him or her to rent a cart instead of walking, or use any other service a golfer is already familiar with and that which goes hand in hand with the game he or she so dearly loves? I once heard, "Don't try to build a watch if you can't even tell time." With that said, let me teach you how to sell a golf membership, golf service, or any golf product professionally.

There are no shortcuts, but there are accelerated learning tools, and in the next chapter, I'll show you how to begin using them and teach you exactly what you need to know to sell any golf product or service. I have done the research for you, I have done the travel, I have invested the money, I have been the one to put everything on the line, and now I have put it all into this book for your consumption. Bon appétit.

CHAPTER 2

LOCKING UP RELATIONSHIPS WITH GOLFERS

The first thing you need to do is get in the right state of mind before going to work and set the tone for the day. Just as athletes warm up before practice or a game, you need to warm up before taking calls or presenting guests. Shit happens, and we all know that, so let's be prepared. There will be days when everything seems to be going wrong, and the last thing you want to do is go into a presentation or speak on the phone when you are not in the zone.

Avoid the Hs: hot and hungry. People get aggravated, irritated, and impatient when they are hot or hungry and tend to lose focus. So make sure you eat a good healthy breakfast before work and dress comfortably but appropriately.

Here are ten exercises and things you can do to prepare yourself for the day and for your presentations:

1. Questions: Every morning I ask myself a series of questions to get focused on the things that are really important to me so that I have a clear direction for the day. You may not be conscious of it, but you ask yourself hundreds if not thousands of questions daily, both good and bad. It is up to you to design questions that will serve you and not hurt you.

For example, ask yourself, "Who am I going to help today? Whose life will I change today? How can I make this the best day ever?"

Don't ask questions like these: Why do I have to work today? When am I going to get what I want in life? Why is my neighbor more successful than I am?

Your brain can answer only the questions you ask it, so choose your questions wisely, and design your questions so that you'll get the answers that will empower you and not depress you—you're the programmer.

Ask yourself questions like these before you go into a presentation: If I don't do my very best for this golfer, how much will it cost me and him or her? How can I make this golfer realize that this is the course where he or she will feel at home? If I half-heartedly go through this presentation and skip steps, will I regret it later? If this golfer leaves the course today without making a commitment, will he or she join my competitor just because I was too lazy to give my very best?

The reason you want to ask yourself great questions is because your brain (which is the most powerful computer in the world) will search for (or direct its focus toward) an answer for the empowering questions. When you are faced with a challenge, you should always ask yourself what is great about it, how you can turn it around to be a valuable tool, and so on. You have the most advanced computer with the fastest search engine known to humankind resting on your shoulders. Start using your computer more effectively by asking yourself empowering questions and focus on what you really want.

2. Posture: The way you carry yourself will affect your attitude. Make sure you stand tall with your shoulders back and your head straight; you are a winner, and winners walk, talk, and carry themselves like winners. Strike the victory pose: put your arms above your head as if you have just won the gold and hold it for sixty seconds. Studies on this pose suggest it really does boost your confidence.

3. Visualization: Imagine going through the day and everyone is smiling and laughing, and you're in control. You are closing every sale, everyone is patting you on the back, you are the envy of everyone, and every new golfer is leaving your office, knowing he or she has just made the best decision of his or her life. Create this image in your mind because your brain doesn't know the difference between what has actually happened and what you are just imagining. Top athletes are known to use this visualization technique in preparation for competition; if Olympians use this technique, you should too.

4. Affirmations: Affirmations are words that you chant over and over to yourself with positivity, intensity, and varying tonality. For example,

you can say, "I am the greatest salesman in the world," "I am a winner," "I always win," or something like "I am a lean, mean fighting machine" (from an old Bill Murray film). The idea is to come up with your own affirmations from your heart that motivate you and say them throughout the day with intensity and conviction.

5. Breathing: Everyone living is breathing, but not everyone knows how to breathe properly. There are a couple of breathing exercises you should be aware of. I learned them in martial arts, and they have a calming effect. First, I take deep breaths as I limber up my body in a tai chi sort of way: I take a deep breath in, hold it, and then exhale as I change my stance, either pushing out, up, in, or down with my hands. The other is to take in four short, fast breaths and exhale four short, fast breaths.

6. Focus: I get perturbed when I hear the label genius thrown around. We can all be geniuses if we just have unwavering focus on any given subject, task, field, endeavor, and so on. People say Michael Jackson was a musical genius; I disagree. I believe people like Michael Jackson, Michael Jordan, and Stevie Ray Vaughan are/were totally focused on their goals and put every ounce of energy and minute of their days into perfecting their love for music, sports, arts, business, sales, marketing, and so on. Focus on your goals, and you can become a genius too.

7. Smile and laugh often: Laughing puts you in a good mood. It is impossible to be sad or angry when you are laughing or smiling. People tend to mirror others, and when you smile, most people will smile back. A simple smile can change your future and the quality of your life.

8. Humming: Hum a familiar tune to eliminate fear and anxiety. Humming distracts the analytical part of your brain, which helps you stop thinking for a minute to clear your head. Also, if you feel nervous, remember to hum sixty seconds before your presentations; you'll forget you are nervous.

9. Calm yourself: A sale is a performance, and the last thing anyone wants to witness is a performer with performance anxiety. You must be in control and confident at all times. One way to calm your nerves is to carry something in your pocket or in your hand that is familiar and comforting. It will calm you and soothe your nerves. It's just like a child with a security blanket.

10. Attire: Always dress for success, which translates into always dressing for your prospects. People like people who look (or dress) like they do. This was very hard for me early in my career when I started consulting because I dressed super smooth. Miami Vice was a show in the early 1980s where the characters dressed really sharp, and I absolutely loved the look and wore it well. Then in the late 1980s, Nike came out with a line of Michael Jordan warm-up suits that were super cool too, and I wore Jordan head to toe, but club owners were more conservative dressers, which meant later in my career, I came to love khakis, button-downs, golf shirts, and blue blazers. So before you leave the house, think of your customers and dress for them, not for yourself. Again, learning the balance is the key to dressing to impress. Never overdress or underdress. Do your best to mirror your prospects or at least your industry.

Once you get to the course, prepare your office for success. Turn your computer on and clean your desk of clutter. Have the files that are relevant to the day's tasks and appointments on your desktop and nothing else. Make sure your office is clean and neat. Cleanliness is extremely important, and that goes for your body, breath, clothes, and office. People who present themselves as sloppy will convey that message to their prospects.

Put a couple of pictures on the wall relevant to your goals—inspirational messages about golf, for instance. But only have a couple; make sure they are not too busy, and keep them on the wall behind you so that your guest's attention will always be forward.

Colors matter; they trigger different thoughts, feelings, and emotions, so learn how to use them to your advantage. The color green is comforting and relaxing. Green signifies that food and water are readily available and relaxes us. I am not a fan of the color green, but I'll use any tool available to me to close a sale. The color of success is red. Red is a powerful color and draws people to you. Ladies, if you want more attention from men, wear red. They will definitely stop and take notice. The color blue is thought to enhance our creativity and is linked to hygiene, water, and purity. Yellow is believed to trigger hunger. This is why most fast-food restaurants have yellow in their logos.

Always offer the prospect something warm, like hot tea or coffee; if the prospect is holding something warm, it will help him or her warm up to you. Getting your prospect to feel positive sensations in your presence is paramount to your success. The three most powerful sensations are warmth, softness, and weight:

- Warmth links our brains to security; yes, a simple cup of coffee or a hot cup of tea can send this sensation to the brain. Now the prospect will begin to let his or her guard down and trust you more.
- Softness is a great way to disarm your prospects to be influenced. Get two soft chairs for your office for prospects to sit on and make sure your chair is hard. People who sit in a hard chair are much tougher negotiators, and since you want to be in charge, don't let yourself get too comfortable.
- Weight is associated with the feeling of quality. Later, when you take the prospect on a tour of the property, you should have him or her swing a club and drive a cart so that he or she will experience this sensation as well.

Now that your office is set up properly for conducting business, start calling to confirm your appointments for the day. The calls should be short and sweet. If the prospect doesn't answer the phone, it is OK to leave a voice mail or send a text message. The call should go something like this: "Hey, Chuck, this is Bob from ABC Golf Course. I just wanted to call and remind you that you are welcome to bring a friend when you visit the course today. I look forward to seeing you at one p.m., have a great morning." Say nothing negative; your words should all be positive. You also could say, "I just wanted to remind you to bring your clubs" (if they think they are just coming to the course for a tour) or anything else just to get them committed to the appointment.

Today's membership directors have it much easier with e-mails and text messages because if you can get the prospect to agree to an appointment in writing he or she is far more likely to show up than if the confirmation was verbal. So use these tools when possible and have your prospects confirm by e-mail or text message so that they are more committed to the appointment.

You must know how to answer the phone properly when receiving an incoming call at the course, handle an information call, and do a proper handoff—turn the guest over to the membership director (a.k.a., sales counselor or salesperson). These three steps are covered in the free download on my website, so make sure you go to www.golfmarket-ingmmc.com.

I have divided my sales system into four phases: interview, tour, close, and future business. I believe most presentations last about an hour, so I want you to think of each section as a twenty-minute session. They say people's minds start to wander after twenty minutes of the same task, and since the goal is to keep our prospects engaged, try to keep each portion to no more than twenty minutes. Of course, there are always exceptions to any rule, and if your prospect is fully engaged, don't worry about the time.

In the interview, you want to probe and ask questions. The more questions you ask, the more information you will have, and as you now know, the person with the most information (and who knows how to use that information) usually wins. This holds true in just about everything in life but especially in sales. The questionnaire flow is paramount, so do your best to keep the prospect in one mind-set at a time. If at all possible, complete all your questions about a specific topic before moving on. Ask the easy questions first. Save sensitive questions for the end when you have already built a rapport with the golfer. Try to set up your questions so that they flow from one to the next seamlessly. Probe for problems, and magnify the pain because later in the presentation you'll want to use that pain as leverage to get the golfer to make a commitment today.

Start looking for signs of the golfer's preferred communication. Is it visual or auditory? Golfers who are visual communicators use their hands a lot. Golfers who are auditory communicators speak loudly, quickly, and with inflections. Learn to speak at the proper pace when presenting, especially with an auditory communicator. It is said that you should speak at a pace of about three and a half words per second to get the best results. If you speak too slowly, you'll sound condescending or slow minded, and if you speak too fast, you risk coming across as untrustworthy. You will see their preferences as you dig deeper into their feelings and emotions during the interview. Once you nail down their preferred methods of communication, start to align your own with your golfers'. People like people who are like them. Care enough to enter into their world.

You also want to determine which social style your golfer has. Is he or she a director, a relator, an analytic, or a socialist? The reason these social styles are so important to understand is because everyone falls primarily into one of these categories, but people do not follow any specific social style 100 percent. For example, your core social style may be that of a director, but as a director, you still have some of the traits of a socialist, a relator, and an analytical.

It's important to understand these four social styles because each golfer you engage in a sales presentation is going to fall into one of them. The more you know about each social style, the better equipped and prepared you will be to accommodate that prospect. One of the first things we learn as children is the golden rule: "treat others the way you want to be treated." I have changed this because I believe you should treat others the way they want to be treated.

What I mean by this is if you are speaking with a golfer whose core social style is that of a director and you approach him or her with a socialist style, the golfer is going to be annoyed because he or she wants you to get straight to the point and not socialize. The same goes if you are trying to lock up a relationship with a socialist; if you approach him or her as a director—straight to the point—the golfer is going to perceive you as being rude and unfriendly and, therefore, will be annoyed by your approach, making it less likely that he or she will want to enter into a relationship with you or your golf course. When you adjust your personality to the golfer, you are not being a phony; you are paying the golfer the highest compliment possible by demonstrating you care enough to enter into his or her world.

Throughout the years of studying the psychology of sales and marketing, I have heard several different variations of this concept of four social styles, and there are numerous labels for each style, depending on the psychologists you are listening to or the book you are reading. I, however, prefer to look at them as the four basic personality types. Again, forget the label because all that matters is that you are familiar with them and their strengths and weaknesses. Below are brief descriptions of the four types.

A director is straight to the point, wants the bottom line, does not waste his or her time, is very impatient, and may come across as arrogant and self-centered.

The analytic wants the numbers, the details, and anything and everything to review; analytical people are normally middle of the road, with few highs or lows.

A socialist loves to socialize. Relationships are extremely important. He or she is a flashy dresser, loves bright colors, has pictures everywhere, and is typically not very organized.

A relator needs to relate to others. He or she considers what everyone else thinks, never wants to upset the norm, and finds it difficult to make decisions independently.

Another great sales tool is to use the prospect's name as much as possible because we associate positive feelings with our names, and our brains light up when we hear them.

The power of eye contact is important as well. Direct eye contact is a tactic for dominance and commands authority. Staring, on the other hand, scares people and makes them uncomfortable, which goes back to the predatory fears of our past. If you are uncomfortable with eye contact, look just above the center of the person's eyes. It appears as if you are looking straight into his or her eyes, but you're not, which will be comforting to you.

There are four phases to my system of locking up relationships with golfers: the interview, the tour, the close, and future business. I am going to walk you through each phase starting with the interview.

Interview

The interview is your time to listen and ask your prospect questions. This is not a time for you to make suggestions, tell your story, give advice, or have any other dialogue. Let the guest talk. Remember, people's favorite subjects are about themselves, their families, their pet projects, and so on. Use this time to get as much information as possible. Your ability to conduct a proper interview will be the key to your success, not only in this area of your business but also in all aspects of your life. We were born with two ears and only one mouth; our creator was trying to tell us something. As in most things, the foundation must be strong enough to build on. The interview is the foundation of the membership sale, and it must be strong enough to support you through each additional phase, all the way to the end of your presentation.

It is imperative you interview guests before you tour them around the property. How else will you know exactly what their interests are? And equally important, how will you know where to start and end your tour? Most novices start the presentation with the tour, which is an ignorant move because the tour needs to be designed around the golfer's wants and needs. Another huge mistake is to have a canned tour. Every tour must be tailored to the prospect's emotions, wants, needs, and social style. Never tour anyone without first sitting somewhere quiet and conducting a proper interview.

Remember, the interview is about asking golfers how they feel about the game, your golf course, and its products and services. Understanding the role psychographics play in the decision-making process is paramount. Uncovering important attitudes, perceptions, beliefs, and behaviors are crucial in the process of locking up the relationship. You want to gather as much information as possible about the golfer sitting in front of you and know exactly what it is that triggered him or her to come to your golf course today. What emotions are driving the golfer to the golf course? Everything you want to know about a golfer can be discovered in the interview. If you uncover the pertinent information, you will definitely lock up that relationship and have a new golfer.

Your primary goal is to get the golfer to associate as much pleasure as possible with being a golfer of your course and associate even more pain with not making the commitment today. But first, you must unearth the golfer's goals, needs, and wants. Show the golfer you truly care; emphasize your concern for his or her goals. You should show all prospects you are committed to helping them achieve their goals, and all this can be accomplished through a properly executed presentation starting with an interview.

I have designed an interview questionnaire called the "Tour Sheet," which you can use to discover guests' goals, wants, likes, and dislikes so that you can show them how your golf course, product, or service can fulfill their needs and wants. I call the interview questionnaire a tour sheet to remind the sales representative to ask the questions first, before taking the guest on the tour of the property. This way the professional salesperson can use the answers as a guide and reminder of the guest's interests throughout the tour. If you haven't downloaded the tour sheet yet, do it now at www.golfmarketingmmc.com. In the download, I cover the tour sheet in detail, so I'll just hit the highlights here to save room for information that isn't covered in the download.

The tour sheet (questionnaire) serves four purposes:

1. Unearth the pain and pleasure the golfer associates to becoming a member.
2. Learn enough about the guest to guide him or her on the correct path to achieve his or her goals.
3. Uncover and be prepared for the golfer's probable objections.
4. Gather the right information to help the golfer make an emotional buying decision today.

Here are the four core objections you'll hear when trying to lock up a relationship with a golfer:

1. Time—I don't know whether I have the time.
2. Money—I don't know whether I can afford it.
3. Spouse—I need to speak with my spouse before making a decision.
4. I need to think about it—I need more information.

Since you are now well aware of the core objections before they even arise, it is up to you to prepare for them. All four of these objections can be easily overcome with logical and emotional reasoning. To overcome these objections, you simply have to ask the right questions and secure the appropriate answers before the objections are even verbalized. There are unlimited objections, but these four are the core objections.

Build rapport with your prospect because people buy products they associate the most pleasure with from the person they feel the most connected with. The same principle applies to pain; people do not buy products they associate with pain (dislike) or from a person they associate pain with or are even just uncomfortable with. Think of a time in your life when you really liked a product or service but did not purchase it just because you didn't connect with the salesperson. The opposite is true as well. I am sure there has been a time in your life when the product didn't give you that wow feeling, yet you still bought it because you had built a rapport with the salesperson. I know it has happened to me. One year early in my career, I was in the Midwest, and my car was getting many miles on it from my travels, so I wanted to buy another one with fewer miles. I saw this beautiful black Mercedes 300E and pulled over. I really liked the car, but the salesman and I just didn't click, so I passed on it. Later that evening, I got a call from the salesman's father, who owned the dealership, and because we hit it off so well over the phone, I purchased the car the following day.

Start building a rapport with the golfer first, before you explode with enthusiasm; later, you will know how to express your enthusiasm once you determine the type of golfer you have in front of you and have gauged his or her level of enthusiasm. You can't start at level ten if your client is at level one; you'll blow him or her out of the water. The same is true if he or she is at level ten and you're at level one; you'll bore the golfer to death. Find common denominators, and align with the golfer/prospective member. People like people who are like them or are how they want to be. When people are dissimilar to each other, they tend not to like each other. If you find yourself in a situation where you don't immediately like a customer, ask yourself what you could like about him or her. First, align with the customer; then, lead the customer.

You must know your product well and be enthusiastic about it and its possibilities, but pace yourself to first gauge your golfer. Building rapport is the easiest part of the presentation; the best way to build rapport is to find a common denominator between you and the customer. Golf is obviously one common denominator, but that's just the beginning. Don't stop there; find more common denominators to make a tighter connection. Other ways of building rapport are to give a sincere compliment, find a common interest, tell a relevant story, and so on. Connect and become his or her best friend. The golfer wants to know what you are really paying attention to: his or her interests or your commission. Remember, the golden rule is wrong. You should do unto others as they would have you do unto them. Building rapport is about the other person, and in sales, your feelings don't matter; the customer's feelings are all that matters.

Learn the art of mirroring. Mirroring builds rapport by getting two people to feel the same emotions. Neurons light up in your brain when you mirror someone or he or she mirrors you, which means we feel what we see—a connection. Engage golfers on their level; use their vocabulary, body language, communication preferences, and social style. Mirroring communicates that you are on the same page, from the same tribe. This goes back millions of years. If someone was different, the members of the tribe feared that the person would compete for their resources, but when someone was the same as the other members of the tribe, everyone tended to stay comfortable.

Try using some of these questions to start building rapport:

1. How long have you been playing the game?
2. How is your golf game right now?
3. How does your game today compare with last year?
4. What part of your game are you struggling with?
5. What are your goals for this year?
6. Are you on track with meeting your goals?

Questions are the greatest friends of a salesperson. By far one of the most important skills that separate professional salespeople from novices is knowing when and how to ask questions. Questions help us get to the deeper levels of attitudes and feelings. They can also bring thoughts and ideas that aren't easily or quickly expressed to the surface. A professional salesperson can probe deeper into every answer the golfer gives by turning it into another question. Probing is learned through trial and error and is best done by feel. When you ask some very simple questions, you will uncover unmet needs, wants, wishes, and desires and then you can present a way for the golfer to meet them and take the presentation to the next level.

It is important you completely understand the principles of pain and pleasure as they relate to people's choices. Everything we do in life boils down to two driving forces: the desire to avoid pain and the desire to gain pleasure. Whether subconsciously or consciously, you are moving either toward pleasure or away from pain. The clothes you wear, the car you drive, the clubs you join, the friends you have, and even things as small as the way you comb your hair are all guided by your association with the pain or pleasure it will bring you.

Unfortunately, people will do far more to avoid pain than they will to gain pleasure. But it is imperative you learn ways to motivate your prospects by using either force. Ask yourself this: Do you tend to do things because it's crunch time (your butt is on the line) or do you tend to jump right in and get things done based on the possibilities (goals and sense of achievement)? If someone tends to wait until the last minute, he or she is likely pain motivated, and if the person tends to jump right in and get things done immediately, he or she is likely pleasure motivated. Your goal is to stimulate the golfer's wants, wishes, goals, and desires and to stir up the golfer's pain of not making a change today while linking enormous pleasure to making a decision today. This is known as the carrot-and-stick method of motivation. Ask the right questions, and you can easily determine which method of motivation your prospect responds to more favorably and shape your presentation around that method.

You should have two types of questions prepared: one set to stir up pain and another set to stimulate pleasure, evoking positive emotions toward your product and services.

Here are some examples:

- Pain: Are you playing the best you can?
- Pleasure: What was your best round ever?

I assure you there was a time when the prospect felt he or she played like a pro; you just need to discover when and bring it to the surface so that he or she can relive that time and experience those feelings now. Think of it this way: Aren't there certain songs that take you back to a certain time, place, and memory and that evoke certain emotions and feelings?

It's a rhetorical question; of course there are. It is your job to take the golfer back in time, whether it was yesterday or twenty years ago, and get him or her to feel those same feelings and emotions right now and link them to your product. The beautiful thing with this technique is that you are the conductor and can choose which feelings and emotions to evoke by the questions you ask.

An undisturbed prospect will not buy your products or services today. Unearth desires that are not being met and pleasures that have been suppressed. Paint a mental picture of exactly what he or she wants, and show him or her the possibilities. Get the prospect to focus on the positive, and make it real. Ask more questions, such as, "If you did achieve your goals in less than three months, would you be happy again the way you were back then? How would that make you feel?" Get his or her imagination to start seeing the mental picture (make it real). Then go back to that throughout the presentation. For example, say something like, "Just picture your perfect game." Whatever someone is thinking about, he or she will feel the emotions associated with that experience. For example: "Tell me the time when you felt the happiest in your life? How did it feel? What were you doing?" Now he or she will start to feel those same feelings. The same principle applies to sadness. Whatever we focus on, that's what we will feel.

Here are a few more sample questions to stimulate pleasure and stir up pain. These questions evoke pleasure:

1. What part of your game would you like to improve over the next ninety days?
2. What part of your game would you change if you could?
3. What do you want to get out of being a member of our golf course?
4. If money were not an issue, what would you want most out of your experience at the club?

And these questions bring up pain:

1. Are you happy playing five- and six-hour rounds at your local public course?

2. What will happen to your game if you don't take action today?
3. How will you feel if you miss out on this opportunity?
4. Have you failed yourself in the past?
5. Are you beating your buddies when you play golf with them?
6. How much do you lose each round?
7. What are your frustrations with your game?

Once you have started to stir up golfers' pain, it is time to relieve them of their pain by demonstrating how your course, product, or service will eliminate all their frustration and have them enjoying their lives, full of energy, and feeling all their past pleasures once again, in just a few short months.

The interview should take about twenty minutes, as I said in the beginning, but do not proceed to the tour until you have the prospect emotionally engaged. If you need more time, take it because this is where you need to have the prospect selling himself or herself on why he or she must join today. It is very important to reiterate that golfers buy for emotional reasons and justify their purchases with logical reasons, so make absolutely sure you have given the golfer enough emotional reasons to justify joining today before going to the next phase.

Tour

The tour is the time to demonstrate how your course has everything needed to achieve the golfer's goals and transfer your enthusiasm to your prospect. Demonstrations always grab people's attention and create interest. Always carry a pen and paper or tablet (refrain from using your mobile to avoid looking unengaged) with you so that you can take notes of your prospect's answers and responses, as well as your observations. You retain only 20 percent of the information you hear and 40 percent of what you hear and what you see, but if you hear, see, and write down the information, your retention goes up to 80 percent.

Always start the tour with the golfer's area of least interest, and end in the area of his or her greatest interest—build up to the climax. Remember, after the tour is done, it's time to do the paperwork (close the sale/lock up the relationship), and you want the golfer enthusiastic when you start that process. Always end on a positive note because the prospect will remember the last part of the tour and conversation more than the beginning or middle; this phenomenon is called the recency effect.

Whatever you do, make sure your statements and facts are consistent throughout your presentation and consistent with those of your coworkers. It's called the consistency principle. When a person hears things that are consistent, his or her brain releases dopamine (the pleasure chemical) and creates a feeling of happiness. However, inconsistency suppresses dopamine, which produces negative feelings. Inconsistency makes us very uncomfortable. In our evolutionary past, inconsistency was very bad, and people who were inconsistent were deemed untrustworthy and, therefore, shunned by the tribe. Our brains developed a way to punish us for being inconsistent. That is why you must always be consistent with your message. It is so deeply rooted in our brains that it will always be a game changer.

The same goes for repetition. People believe a familiar statement after they have heard it at least three times. But don't say it exactly the same way each time; convey the point in three different ways while still saying the same thing. We need consistency in our lives. So design some great statements about your course, and say them consistently throughout the tour.

It is crucial to involve the golfer's five senses (sight, hearing, touch, smell, and taste) during the tour. This will get him or her more connected with the property and, therefore, more excited about becoming a member, which will make your job far easier. The sale is made during the interview and on the tour if you learn how to profile and align with your prospect (i.e., discover communication preference, identify social style, ask all the right questions to stimulate pleasure, stir up pain, and get the prospect's senses involved throughout the tour). The closing will be just a formality.

You must get prospects on the course; get them to grip a club, meet some other golfers, have a drink in the bar, eat a sandwich, meet the cart girl, play a hole, drive a cart, anything and everything that gets their senses engaged—no excuses, just do it. In the health-club business we have the prospective member get on the equipment, put their hand in the pool and Jacuzzi, walk in the sauna, step in the steam room, jump in an aerobics class, and so on, even if the prospect came in the club wearing a business suit or dress. No matter what the situation is, you must find an appropriate way to get the golfer's senses engaged during the tour. The retail industry spends millions of dollars to learn consumers' buying patterns, and they know better than anyone if they can get you to touch a product, you'll probably buy it.

Here is an important note about smell: When a salesperson tries to sell you something and has bad breath or is wearing an obnoxious amount of cologne or perfume, do you buy from him or her? Smell is one of the fastest things that can change a state of mind—for example, take you from being interested to being disgusted. When you are an infant, your sense of smell develops before most of your brain. Some smells trigger disgust (one of the most powerful emotions), and when a prospect is disgusted, game over.

In many instances, people buy based on the emotions and feelings the product will give them, not because of the product itself. If you are excited about a product and convey (transfer) that excitement, the golfer will want those feelings of excitement as well. People will buy whatever the product or service is, provided the product or service can produce the same feelings or emotions. When we feel pleasure, we want to experience it often. The feeling of familiarity takes over and makes us feel good. You must be able to transfer your enthusiasm about golf and your course to your prospective clients.

Be very careful if you have any unresolved concerns or doubts about your product or any aspects of your product because you are certain to unconsciously convey them to the golfer. You better resolve these issues before meeting with any potential golfers. I once read that if you are mad, worried, confused, or in any other negative state of mind or feeling any negative emotions when thinking about your product or service, you will associate those same feelings with that product or service. The opposite is also true: if you are happy, excited, enthusiastic, and so on, you will associate positive feelings with your product and service. When you talk about your product negatively to your spouse or coworkers, you'll link negative thoughts to your product. In some cases, people do this so often they can never sell the product again.

When a golfer starts to focus on the negative or untruths, carefully align with the golfer ("I understand your concerns") and redirect them to the positives ("Let me show you what we have found"). Make absolutely sure before you go on a tour that you are fully prepared to project the exact feelings you must convey to get the desired results. Get your mind focused on the good things in your life, on your products and services, and on the course. It is imperative you are 100 percent confident and enthusiastic when it comes to your product and services.

As you are touring the property, ask a series of questions, but be sure to allow the prospect time to expound on his or her answers. When you are asking questions, learn to pace them so that they don't turn the tour into an interrogation. Below are lists of questions to stir up positive and negative emotions during the tour. I am just giving you a few examples; feel free to rewrite them in your own words, context, and delivery. You should subtly ask your questions throughout the tour; be patient. Make sure you come across as truly interested, and don't let the questions seem intrusive.

Put together some yes questions (questions you know will be answered with a yes) to have some smaller yeses build up to the big yes later in the closing; it's called the foot-in-the-door (FITD) technique. Ask easy yes questions first, like "Isn't it a beautiful day?" Then start working your way up to the big yes, which will be the "Yes, I want the membership to start today!"

The questions below are paired with some core emotions that will always play a role in your sales presentations, so learn how to use them to your advantage. Design as many questions as you can think of to evoke these emotions.

The following list highlights some negative as well as positive emotions we all feel from time to time, which can be used to motivate prospects to make a buying decision today:

- Fear: People are naturally afraid of being left out. Capitalize on this fear, and show the prospects that they must make a buying decision today so that they don't miss out on an opportunity that is available only at your golf course or only today. An example of this is a first-visit incentive: "If you enroll on your first visit, you get X, and I am sure you don't want to miss out on getting X, do you?" Asking questions designed to solicit a no answer can also benefit your presentation. When you ask a question where you want a no answer, shake your head no very inconspicuously, and the prospect will mirror your actions by shaking his or her head and responding with a no answer. It is difficult (unnatural) for someone to say yes when he or she is shaking his or her head no. Use this same technique if you want the prospect to answer yes; move your head up and down to encourage a yes response. If you don't think this technique really works, try it on your family and friends for fun, and you'll be amazed—and amused.

- Frustration: "Do you feel as if you are not achieving your goals because you are not practicing enough or playing enough golf?" Show your prospects how a golf membership will help them achieve their goals because of the unlimited access they will have to the practice range and practice greens if they are members of the course.

- Worry: "Do you worry about your game? Do you worry your skills are deteriorating?" Show prospects how a golf membership will help them eliminate the worry once they take a proactive step by joining today because as a member they will have unlimited access.

- Discontent: "Do you feel envy for other golfers who are living the lifestyle you love?" Show prospects how a golf membership will give them access to a more rewarding lifestyle. Introduce them to golfers who fit the same profile of core and avid golfers, and show them they can socialize with other golfers for motivation and inspiration.

- Anger: "Does your anger due to poor performance on the course agitate you and keep you from playing as well as you should? Do you feel grumpy, bad tempered, and easily annoyed because your game is so volatile?" A golf membership will give you confidence in your game because you will have the opportunity to practice more often and more practice equates to more consistency.

- Regret: "Do you ever feel regret because you haven't devoted the time to the game that you love?" Let prospects know that if they do not buy a golf membership today it will be something they might add to their growing list of regrets.

- Embarrassment: "Do you feel embarrassed when golfing with your buddies because you hit the ball poorly or have a bad slice?" Show prospects how a golf membership can save them from the embarrassment they are feeling right now by getting them to imagine their dream round, and let them know that dream will become a reality much sooner if they get started today.

- Hopelessness: "Do you feel you are drifting aimlessly with your game, without the hope it will get better?" A golf membership will give prospects a new direction and open up new opportunities for them to set goals and improve their game.

- Sadness: "Do you feel sad when you see how you hit the ball? Are you feeling miserable, depressed, and gloomy because of your poor performance?" A golf membership will help prospects meet new people and build new relationships.

- Guilt: "Do you feel guilty because you have neglected your own wants?" You can alleviate those guilty feelings with a golf membership and start living your life to the fullest.

- Achievement: "How does joining the course today contribute to the goals you have set for your game? How would it feel to beat all your buddies and take their money for a change?" Every little step you take to improve your game is considered an achievement.

- Pride: "Wouldn't you be proud to be a member of this course?" Golfers can take pride in being part of a prestigious golf course. They can feel proud they are living the dream. "How proud of yourself will you be when you achieve your golfing goals?" Question: Haven't you heard a golfer brag about being a "member" of such-and-such course when you knew the course was a municipal property that sold season passes and not memberships? Of course you have. Golfers want to belong and take pride in membership.

- Security: "Won't you feel more secure when you're playing a round with coworkers or clients, knowing you are playing your home course?" Design questions to elicit this emotion. For example, how does joining today offer your prospect a sense of security? This is a blanket emotion that includes money, love, acceptance, power, and control.

- Self-improvement: How does joining today appeal to the golfer's sense of self-improvement? "Wouldn't it be great to know you can work on your game anytime you want because you are a member of the course? Are you goal oriented? Is striving to play better important to you?" When you are a member of our course, you become more confident because you'll see results.

- Status: How does a golf membership contribute to the status of your prospect? Does being a member of a golf course make him or her feel important? By looking successful in the eyes of their peers, golfers will feel more significant. "What do you think your coworkers will say when they see you are now a member of this course? Won't it be great when you have priority over public play when reserving your tee-times?"

- Ambition: How does a golf membership help the prospect get more out of life and get ahead? Ask your prospect, "Are you in business? Do you entertain clients? Are you looking for a new career? A golf membership will put you side by side with some of the community's top executives. Did you know that corporations look at an applicant's lifestyle when choosing who best fits the company's long-term goals?"

- Power: In what ways does a golf membership offer prospects more power or control over their lives? A golf membership will give prospects a new perspective on life, satisfying all six core emotional needs (certainty, variety, significance, love and connection, growth, and contribution), while giving them the power to feel in control of their lives. "Don't you think being a member of this course will give you more power and control over your life?"

By this time, you should already have the pertinent information you need to get the prospect to make the buying decision today. The prospect must have enough wants and justifications as to why he or she must buy now, and if he or she doesn't, you did a poor job on the interview and tour.

You must learn to pick up on body language that can tell you when prospects are ready to buy: facial expressions, posture, vocabulary, and actions. For example, if prospects' facial muscles are tight (not in irritation but because they are in deep thought) and if they are scratching their chins, they are giving the decision great thought. The more relaxed the golfers are, the closer to buying they are. If you put something like a brochure or contract in front of your prospects and they start touching it or asking questions about it, they are more likely to say yes. If golfers are smiling a little more often than they had in the beginning of the presentation, their attitudes are friendly and they are aligning with you. They are probably ready to buy. If the golfers are excited, their eyes will open a little wider and their pupils will slightly dilate. If the golfers are leaning forward, they are listening more intently; they are really attentive and interested in what you have to say and will ask questions. All these tells signal that golfers are ready to buy. You must watch for these signs and take the appropriate action: lock up the relationship, and close the sale.

Closing

Always go into the closing phase by knowing where you stand. Is the prospect hot or cold? Take his or her temperature by asking test-closing questions. Test-closing questions are opinion-asking questions; opinion questions are not decision-making questions. Start with a question like "In your opinion, do you feel enrolling today would be the best first step toward reclaiming your game?" By test closing, you avoid overselling, such as selling the membership during the interview and tour and then buying it back (buying it back is a sales term for not knowing when to shut up, which can cost you a sale and, therefore, a missed opportunity to earn a commission).

Here are three test-closing questions:

1. How long have you been considering enrolling in a golf membership? (You are not asking the prospect if he or she wants to join today; you are just digging deeper to see if he or she has already formed an opinion about enrolling anytime in his or her life.)
2. If you can play unlimited golf for X, is it worth it to you?

3. I know you are concerned about _____, but wouldn't it be worth _____ to get _____ (some benefit)? (The benefit must be strong enough to provide leverage to move them away from their fears.)

Test-closing allows you to shed light on the nos—for example, "No, I don't want to buy" and "No, I'm not ready now"—and overcome them before they are verbalized. Do not hide from nos; everyone will get them, so welcome them. This far into the presentation, the nos are easy because they're "not yets," and you're not asking prospects to buy now; you're just finding out what they're thinking at this point. Don't use the shotgun approach and try to attack every objection head-on. Use test-closing questions to get those objections out so that you can take them out like a fine-tuned sniper—one at a time.

If you're always test-closing, you'll know what kind of state of mind the prospect is in. Observe if you're moving him or her toward or away from a commitment. If he or she is moving in the wrong direction, make a change in your presentation. Never ask the customer to buy until you are positive he or she is ready. You accomplish this, of course, through test closing. This helps you and your ego as well because you never feel rejected and are always comfortable and confident throughout the presentation.

Here are some more test-closing questions:

1. If you were to go ahead with a golf membership, when would you want it to start? (This question is designed to see if the prospect has formed an opinion on joining today or is still procrastinating.)
2. If we were able to overcome _____, would you be ready to move forward today?
3. Does this membership package sound like it will meet your needs?

When you feel the golfer is ready to join, assume the close/go for the close (assuming the close means the prospect has already given you the go-ahead with the membership whether verbally or nonverbally) by moving right into the paperwork. I prefer go for the close opposed to "assume the close" because I never assume anything, but it is an industry term, so I would be remiss if I didn't teach it to you.

Even though the entire sales process should have been completed during the interview and tour, you may still get some pushback during the paperwork. Do not panic; you should only panic if you have failed to lay the groundwork. Objections are just a cry for more information; celebrate objections. When golfers raise objections, it means they're interested but need more information. Objections at this point are no problem because now you know what is stopping the golfer from making the commitment. Now you know what direction to go in and where to build more value or eliminate pain.

Most objections are questions in disguise, begging to be answered. When you uncover an objection that you have no control over as a salesperson—course conditions, amenities, equipment, scheduling—find a way to brag about it or overcome it. For example, if your property hosts many events, present that as a positive: "Our golfers love this course so much, they want us to host all their events here."

Here are some other ways of handling objections. Always remember that questions are a salesperson's best friend, so learn to use them to overcome objections. Never argue or go against what golfers say or feel. Always align with them. Always answer the questions presented to you. Some salespeople follow the school of thought that you can ignore questions and they will disappear, but I believe all questions should be addressed now so that there is no buyer's remorse tomorrow. Turn an objection into a question. For example, when prospects say, "It's too expensive," ask them, "Can you tell me the reason why you think it costs too much?" Questions are powerful; ask questions that make prospects focus on benefits opposed to their concerns.

Here are a few examples of how to turn objections into questions. Use any of the four objections (time, money, spouse, or "I need to think about it") or insert your own:

- In spite of _____, isn't it possible you can still get enormous value from our membership? Don't you think you can still achieve _____ (the prospect's goals) by being a member?

- How can we get _____ (benefit) without your game having to continue suffering?
- How do we _____ so that you can still benefit from joining today?
- Wouldn't it be great if we could find a way to accomplish _____?
- Do you no longer worry about _____?
- Why would _____ even be an issue since you've been telling me how desperate you are for a change?

Turn the objection back to the prospect. If he or she says, "I don't have the money," then respond, "That's exactly why you must buy it today. You will save an enormous amount of money if you enroll today, and as everyone knows, money saved is money earned."

Overpower objections like "I need to think about it" by piling on more and more reasons why he or she must buy now, for example, because he or she has already been thinking about it for years.

Some of the question examples given in this book are never going to feel comfortable to you. These questions are just examples. You must design your own questions that fit your social style so that you can ask them with conviction. Don't read these examples and say, "I could never say that." Ask yourself, "How can I ask that question in a way that suits my style, or what would be a better question for me to ask than that?"

Move to make an objection a final objection—for example, "If we can agree on X, are you ready to move forward to the paperwork?"

After overcoming the objection and getting positive feedback from the prospect, go for the close. Congratulate the prospect on making a wise decision, and shake hands with him or her. Take out the agreement (contract), and start filling it out.

Go for the close by asking, "How would you like to take care of your membership today: Visa or MasterCard?" Too many options are too confusing—avoid brain overload! Limit the options to two choices. Less is more. Lots of options confuse people, and they will opt not to choose at all. Too many choices tax the lazy brain. Your brain is always looking for ways to conserve energy because it functions on only twelve watts of power. That is why it is difficult for people to make a choice or decision if there are too many options. Reduce the possibilities of confusion by limiting the choices. Make it easy to buy today.

Don't say another word when you ask your closing question; remember, a closing question is a make-a-decision question. If you wait for the customer to answer, he or she will, and it will probably be one of your choices, for example, Visa or MasterCard; if you speak first, you start the entire sales process over. Sometimes the silence will seem to last like an hour. Just be patient and wait; you'll be very happy you did. Whoever speaks first will lose. Remember, by losing (speaking first), the prospect wins because now he or she will stop procrastinating and start a new way of life today. The only acceptable pressure in a professional sales presentation is silence; use it.

After finalizing the paperwork, you must create a compelling future for the new member. Have the new golfer explain to you how he or she plans on changing his or her life since the golfer has now joined the course. Ask him or her, "A year from now, what do you think will stand out as being one of the best things that came from you enrolling today?" Now the new golfer will be able to justify the purchase when talking to his or her peers, spouse, kids, and so on so that he or she doesn't get any pushback.

Always give a gift at the close to induce reciprocation. It always makes someone feel committed. Give a logo cap, logo towel, logo golf ball, free weeklong unlimited range pass, or anything of value at the contract signing. After giving the new golfers (tangible) gifts, do you think they will ever back out? Unlikely. It's called the rule of reciprocity; you give them a logo ball, and they give you their loyalty.

Future business/Buddy referrals

Convert this new relationship into future business. Ask the new golfer before he or she leaves to fill out a buddy-referral sheet (this is part of the free download). If you feel it is necessary, offer him or her something in return. Get as much info on the referrals as possible. Even after presentations you don't close, get referrals. Say to the prospects who choose not to join, "I understand you feel this may not be the right fit for you at this time. Do you know of someone who could benefit from our membership?" Sometimes, prospects will be glad to give you someone else because they'll feel they are no longer in your crosshairs. This theory is called "see a shark, stab your dive buddy."

Between what you have learned here today and what you'll receive in the free download, you will be able to confidently sell any golf product or service to any prospect in the world. If you have comments, please feel free to e-mail me at chuck@chuckmmc.com or chuck@chuckthompson. guru.

Chapter 3 is going to take you to the next level. I share the fundamentals of marketing and lead generation to guide you through several ways to generate revenue for yourself as well as your owner. Growing a business can be one of the most rewarding things you'll do in life, but just like farming, there is a season for planting and a season for harvesting. Professional marketers know how to develop a marketing strategy that will provide the business with revenue year round, which is something all of you must learn as well to grow your businesses, but there is only one way to eat an elephant and that is one bite at a time.

Now that you have learned an ironclad system to lock up relationships with golfers, it is time for you to take the next step and learn the easiest low-cost ways on how to get golfers through the door. Chapter 3 will give you the tools to do just that.

CHAPTER 3

GOLF-MARKETING ESSENTIALS

I
n this chapter I am going to share a dozen of the low-cost ways I used to grow the clubs I represented in the beginning of my career. These tools will be great for you too to generate revenue for your golf course or your golf product. I decided it would be best to write this chapter by reviewing the lowest-cost marketing tools possible—prospecting and lead generation. I am going to discuss the old as well as the new tools for bringing in business, because when your livelihood and the financial health of your business depend on your ability to generate revenue, you'd better have some inexpensive ways to do it. We will also look at the least expensive ways to market your golf course, using tools like the Internet and ending with mail-outs. I will give you the pros and cons of each media and platform while teaching you some practical (real-world) applications for all of them. This way you can hit the ground running no matter what the limitations of your budget may be.

This chapter contains probably the most important tools and resources for those of you just starting your career and business or are operating a business, because you can always assume there is no—or at best, a very limited—marketing budget. By coming into a situation with your eyes wide open and with no expectations of help, you'll be prepared for any scenario. Growing the business is the bottom line. The tools I have laid out in this chapter are inexpensive, proven, and reliable. Just do your best every day to plant the seeds for generating leads, and I promise you, just as with compound interest, your compensation for your efforts will multiply beyond your wildest expectations. When I first started my consulting career, I had no idea how to implement and manage, much less pay for, a full-scale campaign; I busted my butt every day to bring in every single dollar from hard work and determination. I am very fortunate, though, because I love learning, and I always find a way to have fun, even during the difficult times doing the most mundane tasks. The first rule of thumb is ABP: always be prospecting. It's a play on the ABCs of sales: always be closing. Until you have warm bodies in front of you, it's impossible to be closing. Start by having specific prospecting goals, and work your way backward through your numbers.

For example, I need to make five sales this week. If my closing ratio is 10 percent of the people I see, then I need to get in front of fifty people this week. If I work five days per week, I need ten solid appointments per day—it's simple math. I can assure you if you consistently have ten confirmed appointments every day, your sales will be far greater than five per week because your closing percentage will skyrocket with all the practice. It's like anything else in life: the more practice you put in, the better you will inevitably become.

Here are twelve low-cost ways to generate revenue:

1. Buddy sheet: Hands down, the easiest, cheapest, and fastest tool is your buddy sheet (or referral sheet). The buddy sheet is designed to help you get contacts with minimal effort. The majority of the work is already done while the process of giving referrals is simplified for the golfer. The buddy sheet has a list of potential referrals: best friend, brother, sister, aunt, uncle, church friend, and so on. The form is designed this way because when people are approached by someone for a referral they tend to have a mental hiccup and can't (or don't want to) think of anyone. The buddy sheet takes the thinking out of the equation because it reminds prospects of their friends, neighbors, relatives, and so on.

Most membership directors think of getting referrals only after a sale. I think of getting referrals anytime I speak with anyone. As I said earlier, I built my initial reputation on consistently doubling or tripling a club's gross with no marketing or advertising budget whatsoever. Owners seldom hire a consultant when things are going well; sadly, they are more likely to wait until the business is knocking on death's door. So asking for a marketing budget was out of the question. As I honed my skills, I designed all my campaigns around self-funding principles to prove my value to an owner.

The reason I tell you this is because I want you to understand getting referrals was the very first thing I did when I went into a new health club, and it didn't cost me a dime. I would always pick up five or ten memberships in just the first day or two and blow everyone's mind. It was as though two audiences were watching two different movies in the same theater. The other salespeople were captivated by what I was accomplishing, and I was horrified by their not doing the same thing a long time ago.

I would simply photocopy a stack of the buddy sheets and stand at the front desk where members checked in. I would smile, introduce myself, welcome them to the club, hand them the sheet, and say, "Please fill this out, and I will give your friends a free one-week pass to train with you." Pros can easily do the same thing. Every time they check a golfer in, they can introduce themselves, give the golfer a buddy sheet, and tell him or her that he or she will receive a free bucket of balls, a logo ball, a logo cap, or whatever for participating in the Ambassador program.

I did not ask people, "Will you fill it out?" This would have given them the opportunity to say no. I also didn't want them to feel as though they were doing me a favor; I wanted them to know I was doing them a favor by giving them a gift just for participating.

At the end of my first day, I would have hundreds of people to call the following day. Today, it is so much easier with text messaging (SMS), which is one of the best platforms for staying in touch with prospects in today's world because everyone carries a mobile device. There are stats that say almost 80 percent of all text messages are read. MMC®'s studies show the real number to be closer to 70 percent, but that is still huge. The downside of SMS is building a prospect list, since it is an opt-in form of marketing, which means you can't buy a list of prospects and must build your list organically. However, for confirming appointments and following up on previous conversations there is no better platform. The great thing about the buddy sheet is that you are getting the numbers from family members and friends, so start building your SMS list today.

Another thing about the buddy sheet is that normally a couple of the contacts are very good leads. It is so true that birds of a feather flock together. Most people tend to socialize with people in the same income bracket; people who love football tend to socialize with others who love football, and so on.

Buddy sheets can also be useful in a variety of other ways. You can go to all the businesses around your course, hand them out, and tell everyone who fills it out that five good names along with his or her contact information will bring them a free bucket of balls, a logo ball, a free lesson (fifteen minutes), and so on. Of course, you better get this strategy approved by your higher-ups beforehand. Again, not all these leads might pan out, but every time a guest comes to the course asking for you personally, you have another opportunity to make more money. This also gives you the chance to sell the guest or golfer a membership by giving him or her a special offer or discount, like a first-visit incentive, for trading in the pass and joining today; you may waive the enrollment fee if he or she chooses to join today.

Of course, the most obvious way to use a buddy sheet is after a sale, while the new golfer is still on an emotional high from taking the first step of joining your course's program, whether it was buying a membership, preferred player's card, punch card, and so on. Just understand that the only limit to a buddy sheet is the limitation of your imagination. Coworkers will look at you funnily in the beginning when they first see you using these techniques to get referrals, but later, they will ask you for advice. Never follow the herd; they will take you straight to the slaughterhouse. Always think outside the box, and go for it!

Even if you are unable to close a sale (lock up the relationship), after the presentation, ask for referrals. In most cases, people will gladly give you a name or two, thinking they are refocusing your attention on someone else. Either way, it's a win-win.

2. Guest passes: Wow, again, what a wonderful time to be in the golf industry! Back in the day, I had to jump in my car and drive across town to a commercial printer, look through a catalog, pick the font and style of the business card I liked, go back in three days to approve the layout, go back yet again for corrections if needed, and finally go back in a week or two to pick up the cards. Today, you can print high-quality business cards in the comfort of your own home, and if you don't have a personal printer, you can go to a quick-print shop and have them printed and in your hands within an hour.

In the golf business, your business card and free-bucket-of-balls card should be one and the same. Print as many as you can afford, and print "one free bucket of balls" (or whatever free) on the back in bright-red letters, along with an expiration date. Carry a bunch of cards in your pocket at all times. Give one to everyone you meet; everyone loves to get something free. This is a great way to socialize as well. When you meet people, introduce yourself, and let them know you work at a golf course nearby and would be happy to give them a free lesson or bucket of balls; everyone loves the word free, especially if the free product or service has real monetary value.

It is very important to include an expiration date to create a sense of urgency. Most people have a tendency to put off until tomorrow what they could have (or should have) done today. We live in a world of procrastinators. Unfortunately for them, but fortunately for us (professional salespeople), they need someone to help them realize their own inner motivations to get started today. There have been numerous studies done on scarcity and how it gets people to take action. For example, if there is only one item left, everyone wants it. But if the item is plentiful, people will say to themselves, "I'll get one later."

When you go to the market, car wash, gas station, restaurant, and so on, you should be handing out guest passes. Every time you give one out, always put the person's name and expiration date on the pass and then put his or her name, expiration date and mobile number in your lead folder on your smartphone. I cannot express how important building a database of potential clients really is.

Another way to use your business cards is after every sales presentation. I say "every" sales presentation because people tend to forget referrals and future sales from the prospects who do not buy (a.k.a., prospects who walk). Every prospect you visit with should walk away with two guest passes, and you should walk away with two fresh leads. Some people will not want the paper in this paperless world, but you should always have cards readily available because they will at least give you something tangible to hand your prospects. Also, have guest passes on your smartphone so that you can Bluetooth them to prospects as well.

So far, I have talked about two fantastic ways to get started on generating sales with just a couple of bucks invested in paper and ink. Now that you have sold a couple of memberships, lessons, products, services, gadgets, or whatever, it's time you started investing in your future. Again, I will start out with low-budget ways of generating leads before we discuss costlier mediums.

3. Lead boxes: Lead boxes are also called registration boxes. I know some of you out there are going to think these three resources (i.e., buddy sheets, guest passes, and lead boxes) are old school, and they are, but they work. If you want to be great, you have to be willing to do the things others won't, old school or new. I must also warn that the laws have changed drastically since I was in the field using lead boxes, and you must check with your course's owner (and he or she with an attorney) on the current laws regarding this matter. I know there will definitely be a ratio of winners based on the number of registrants. Back in the day, some owners used to put pictures of tropical settings on their boxes that read, "Win a free trip to the Bahamas." That was totally misleading because those trips were set up by real-estate companies selling time-share condo units. The winners had to sit through a weekend-long sales presentation instead of spending all day in the sand as they had hoped. When I put out lead boxes on my own, I just used a picture of a sexy girl and guy on the top and wrote, "Win a free one-year membership," and I always got a great response.

If you're working for a course, ask the owner to buy a hundred boxes for the business; they're very cheap, and they pay high dividends. If the owner buys them, of course he or she will put the course's logo and name on them, and they will be his or her property. If he or she will not buy them, get permission in writing to do it yourself, and ask whether you can get a higher commission on your sales to offset your investment. The worst thing the owner can say is no, but you'll never know until you ask. If you buy the boxes, they're your property, and you can design them however you wish. If I were a pro, I would just buy a picture of a family golfing from iStock or a company like that and put "Win a free golf membership" at the top. You can give all the registrants a free round during the slowest time of the day or even a free fifteen-minute lesson. Don't include the course's name or logo unless it's easy to change; this way, if you leave or buy your own course, you will have a head start on your marketing materials.

The most important things to remember with lead boxes are the three laws of real estate: location, location, and location. Map out your marketplace, and find the top-fifty locations with the highest volume of traffic (preferably related to golf); then make a list of the second highest, third highest, and so on. Then call each store to get the GM's name and schedule.

Next, load your car up with the boxes on your days off, and drive to the businesses (or walk if you have to—I did when I first started). Most people will tell you to call to set up an appointment first, and I agree it would be more polite, but the reality is that most people will tell you no over the phone as a knee-jerk response before they even hear your proposition. I repeat: put the boxes out on your days off. You don't want to leave the course on workdays because you could miss a sale.

Walk into the store carrying the box in your arms, where everyone can see (preferably wearing your logo shirt), and ask to speak to the GM. I used to wear my uniform almost every day, not just because I was poor, although that may have been a contributing factor. We had these cool dark-blue silk Adidas warm-up suits (remember this was in the early 1980s), and I bought one for every day. I got the idea because when I went to lunch someone would inevitably ask me about the health club after seeing the logo on my name tag, and I generated a ton of leads this way. My coworkers thought I was crazy for keeping my name tag on, but I didn't care about what they thought; they weren't paying my bills. They would barely wear their name tags inside the club because they thought they were too cool for name tags. I thought they were being silly because it cost them business.

After being introduced to the manager of the store where you want to place your lead box, let him or her know the purpose of the visit. Explain that you would like to put a registration box near the entrance or exit so that all the store's customers can receive a free "whatever" at the course and that, just for letting you do this, you'll give him or her a free "whatever" for as long as the box stays in the store and is producing. Make sure the managers understand (and you do too) they are VIPs as far as you are concerned, and you plan on taking very good care of them when they are at your course. You must take good care of the GMs who say yes because their experiences at your course will motivate them to generate tons of business for you by encouraging their patrons to register.

Now is a great time to introduce the fact that there are seven basic things on most people's minds when conducting business or listening to business presentations:

1. What is the product or service?
2. What's in it for me?
3. What problem will it solve?
4. What's your proof?
5. Do I need it now?
6. Why do I need the product or service now?
7. What emotional need will the product or service fulfill?

I have said the following many times, and I will repeat it throughout this book: People buy for emotional reasons and justify their purchases with logical reasons. So give the GM numerous emotional reasons to partner with you, such as connection, importance, and contribution, and by giving all his or her customers a free "whatever," he or she can logically justify displaying the box. Don't expect everyone to say yes, because not everyone will. Sales is a numbers game; that's why I told you to start with your A prospects (top fifty), then B (second fifty), C (third fifty), and so on. If you have twenty boxes to put out in a day, you might have to visit two hundred stores, but if you are persistent and do your homework, you will succeed.

After collecting your leads, call all the registrants and invite them in for a free "whatever." I always had several guys and gals around the course who loved training people but hated the sales process, so I would make a deal with them where I would set up potential members with training appointments during the trainers' downtimes, and they would train my prospects for one thirty-minute session for free. This was a win-win-win for everyone. The prospect received a personal-training session (with a value of at least twenty dollars), the trainer had a new prospect, and I sold another membership. If you are the club pro, you can give free fifteen-minute lessons. If you have an assistant pro, he or she can give the free lessons, and if you are the manager, you can set times aside to have your head pro give the lessons. The idea is to always have new bodies on the property.

4. Cold calls: Cold calling is also called telemarketing or dialing for dollars. The laws regarding telemarketing have changed dramatically as have those for lead boxes, so be sure to check with your course's owner or attorney before you start dialing for dollars. In the old days, sales counselors could grab the white pages (yellow pages were for business listings and white pages were for residential listings) and just start hammering out calls. The phone companies even had little neighborhood directories so that salespeople could stay within their market; of course, all this research to find local residents' telephone numbers can be done online now. I use the word we loosely because most membership counselors hated to get on the phone to make cold calls. I never understood their reluctance. I would hear them complaining about their car payments, their rents being past due, and their lack of sales, yet they would just cry on the shoulder of whoever would listen instead of picking up the phone. The least painful way to make cold calls is to start by getting every visiting golfer's name and mobile number to the course. Then you can make courtesy calls just to say hi and see how their rounds went.

All sales-training methods will tell you to qualify the prospect: First, does he or she have the money to buy a membership? Does he or she fit the profile of someone you want as a golfer of the course? Later, we will go into detail about prequalifying prospects before investing advertising dollars, but for a staff member new to the business, you just need warm bodies in front of you, and for now, you'll have to do your own qualifying with good judgment.

The fastest way to qualify prospects is through profiled mailing lists. If you have a budget, I strongly suggest this route because it will save you countless hours of wasted time on the phone. Mailing lists can be compiled from thousands of different sources for thousands of different list profiles. Lists are available for individuals, organizations, and businesses. With individuals, there are a tremendous number of choices available, such as average household income, head-of-household age, type of home, date the home was built, date the home was last sold and for how much, home value, mortgage holders, families with children living at home, number of occupants in the household, number of occupants under the age of eighteen, gender, hobbies, interests, sports played, magazine subscriptions bought, donor activities, mail-order buyers, credit-card purchases, and many other options, making the choices in lists virtually limitless.

For example, MMC® pulls hundreds of lists and combines multiple lists to identify qualified consumers who fit our profile, which is specifically designed to target the casual and nongolfer segments based on geographic, demographic, and psychographic data and tracks those results to know what works best (got the best response). We also track what generates the very best type of business (most revenue, best prospect, and so on) and what gives us the very best ROI for our marketing dollar. This ROI is learned through mistakes and success. The key is to track all the results, not just the responses. Just like many things in life, you get better at something the more you do it, the more information you have, and the more you understand what works and what doesn't.

Never try to sell anything over the phone (unless that's the primary way your product or service is sold), but the appointment is the rule to remember when cold calling; this is where I think novices get discouraged. People get caught up in long conversations on the phone and end up justifying their products or services instead of getting the consumer excited about an appointment. It is difficult (not impossible) to get prospects' emotions and senses engaged over the phone, but if they're face-to-face in your pro shop, it is easy. So get them off the phone and into the pro shop.

There are cold calls made by machines called robocalls. During any election year, you will receive these at your home, but only politicians and emergency agencies are allowed to use them. There have been numerous laws passed lately with huge fines for robocalling people on their home phones, and now some states have even made it illegal to robocall mobile phones. Stay far away from this type of telemarketing because you will regret it.

5. Corporate cold calls: Dialing for dollars can also be used to grow relationships with local businesses. Call them, and invite them in for a free company golf clinic for all their employees or executives. It can be set up as a field trip or company function. It can be presented to the employees as a gift from their company, earning goodwill for the employer. I hope I do not need to say it again at this point, but you will be building your list of prospects with every contact you make.

Before you start making your calls, do your homework:

- Know who the prospect is, and get as much information as possible about the prospect, which is a little more difficult when you're dialing for dollars just to get appointments, but when you're calling businesses, you need to get to the decision makers and get their attention immediately.

When speaking with your prospects, identify ASAP whether they are the decision makers or gatekeepers. If they are the gatekeepers (usually these are secretaries who block unwanted calls, including sales calls) or not the decision makers, direct your presentation to their needs as well as their bosses' since this is a bridge you must successfully cross before getting to the decision maker.

Anticipate some of their wants, needs, and pain points. What are their interests? Most secretaries know more about their bosses' schedules than their bosses do. Secretaries are the perfect candidates for flowers, candies, Christmas cards, birthday cards, and e-mails; add them to your Facebook, Snapchat, Twitter, and other social-media accounts. You must get on the secretaries' good sides because they will be the ones to get you in front of their bosses.

Another option (if you have the money) is to buy a business list for your area from a list company. Some of the most common ways business lists can be generated are by number of employees, amount of annual sales, type of business, branch or home-office locations, contact names, and many other segments.

- Learn as much as possible about the person you will be meeting before you go to the appointment. This is especially important for corporate cold calls. Find something you have in common, like an interest in sports, cars, food, or arts. Discover what you like about the person you're meeting so that you can pay him or her a sincere compliment. Make a list of questions you can ask before arriving for the appointment, both pain and pleasure questions.

The more questions your prospect asks about your golf course, the more interested he or she is. The same goes for you too: the more relevant questions you ask your prospects, the more interested you will seem. Take a few minutes, write down a bunch of questions to ask your prospects that are relevant to their likes and dislikes, and put them in your quiver to use in future conversations; I promise they will serve you well.

Think of and address the prospects' wants and needs. If you address their needs, they will take the conversation to the next level. When probing, always remember prospects' first answers may be knee-jerk reactions, such as, "I don't have the time to play golf," but a couple of follow-up questions may reveal the true reason for the pushback.

When you are preparing to make your calls, prepare yourself for rejection. It is an inevitable fact of life, especially in sales. The greatest ballplayers of all times get hits about every three times at bat, and the greatest salespeople close about the same percentage of cold-call prospects. You are not a professional cold caller, so don't beat yourself up if you can't close 30 percent of your calls. The easiest way to avoid rejection is to never go for the hard close. What I mean by this is constantly build value and ask test-closing questions along the way. For example, start with "Which day of the week is best for you and your executives?" as opposed to "Do you want to buy a corporate membership?" If you go for the hard close, you will get a hard yes or no answer, and if it is no, you will be fighting an uphill battle, but if you're just test closing, you will know whether your prospect is hot or cold.

Another reality you will run into is that some of your prospects will already be golfers of another golf course. This is a golden opportunity for you to learn all about the competition. What does the prospect like most and dislike most about his or her home course? Align with what he or she likes, and show how your golf course is completely different in reference to the bad, but never bad-mouth the competition. No one is interested in being told he or she made a stupid decision by joining another golf course. Just highlight the things you do that no one else does or the things your golf course does better than any other course, such as providing unparalleled customer service.

- Be prepared for objections. Have a minimum of six rebuttals for every possible objection. Know all the possible objections, write down your rebuttals, and commit them to memory. Make it a game and be excited to overcome objections.
- Expect the best; prepare for the worst. Be able to adjust. People will cancel appointments. People won't always do things your way. If someone cancels an appointment, be flexible. Prepare for inevitable setbacks.
- Create demand. It is absolutely imperative there be a demand for your golf product or service and the prospect be aware of that demand.

You need at least ten benefits a prospect will get by giving you an appointment, just as you need ten benefits a golfer will get by joining your golf course today and ten reasons your product is worth ten times more than your membership rates or green fees.

Outline your phone presentation, and set your goals. I scheduled cold calls for times when I couldn't be doing something that paid bigger and faster dividends. It will be necessary to track your responses from all your efforts to gauge the immediate return on investment (your time). I say this because cold calls are on the lower rung of the ladder for me. I prefer face-to-face meetings, but I also know that sometimes I must step out of my comfort zone to grow and get better, so I try everything.

Set specific goals for your phone calls, and stick to your game plan. For example, gather information, build rapport, and set an appointment.

When calling a prospect to set an appointment, follow these three easy steps:

1. Let the prospect know what's in it for him or her.
2. State the emotional and logical reasons for which he or she should meet with you.

3. Give examples of the pain he or she may be experiencing and the pleasure associated with your golf product or service, and explain how it will either alleviate or eliminate his or her pain.

When setting an appointment, ask for only ten minutes of his or her time, and guarantee that if he or she is not fully interested in what you have to say, you will not take up any additional time. Everyone can find ten minutes in a day, but no one has twenty minutes. Start with, and be happy with, ten minutes; don't worry, because if he or she likes what you have to say, time will never be an issue.

How many appointments do you want, and how many calls will it take for you to get that number of appointments? What is your hook to get your foot in the door? For example, "I want to give your executives a free whatever." What area will you call, and what time would be best for calling? What message will you leave if you get a voice mail? You should have a plan to achieve all goals. The next step is to implement your plan and then adjust to unforeseen challenges. Once you have planned and are prepared, go for it!

6. Comarketing strategies: Partner with your local chamber of commerce or other organizations to offer special discounts for their members: police departments, fire departments, municipalities, teachers' unions, and so on. Develop a great corporate offer (using volume pricing); contact all the people you can; and ask them to send out e-mails, put inserts into their newsletters, and put the offer on their Facebook page or any other platform used to stay in contact with members, associates, or affiliates. Make sure your offer is a real value and is a win-win across the board.

7. Social-media platforms: Using social media is paramount for any business, especially businesses that have a social component to them. Facebook's pros: Facebook (FB) can get enormous traffic if it is marketed properly. Your FB friends' list is another marketing list. FB advertising is cheap and easy. It allows you to post ads even without a website.

Facebook's cons: FB has low conversion rates for e-commerce because people use FB to communicate with their friends and loved ones and are not expecting to read your ads. Ad clutter is a problem because FB allows almost everyone to post ads; your ads may be posted with other irrelevant ads. It is hard to capture your audience's full attention since they are chatting, playing, or doing other activities on FB.

One of the other big selling points of FB's paid ads is that they allow you to profile your targets. This is extremely misleading. FB's profiling is rudimentary at best, providing you only four parameters to profile your prospects.

1. Geographic (fantastic, but many people who sign up for an FB account give false information to avoid scammers)
2. Gender (fantastic, but many people who sign up for an FB account give false information to avoid scammers)
3. Age (fantastic, but many people who sign up for an FB account give false information to avoid scammers)
4. Interests (fantastic, but many people who sign up for an FB account give false information to avoid scammers)

You might think you are advertising to a beautiful brunette with a big smile when you are really targeting a blue-haired seventy-year-old with no teeth (FB profiles are notoriously filled with false information). "You get what you pay for" is a saying that resonates for a reason: minimal investments bring less than minimal returns.

Twitter's pros: Twitter allows you to communicate to a large group of people with one message. It is great as a quick communication platform to promote the content of your golf course. It is the simplest to use of all social-media platforms. It's absolutely free.

Twitter's cons: There is a limit to the characters allowed, which limits your message. Not all people use or understand Twitter. Twitter can be distracting.

I chose to highlight just FB and Twitter as examples, but there are hundreds of social-media platforms. Most of them don't provide enough benefits to justify the time or the effort needed to sign up with them. As far as producing any measurable results when it comes to growing your golf course, well, let's just say you have to be patient—it's going to take a while.

You get what you pay for in life; you get back what you put out, and so on. If you are looking to find free golf-marketing platforms, there are some out there. But if you are looking to launch a golf-marketing campaign to grow your business, you might want to look at media and platforms that are going to produce the desired result.

Social media is great for what it is, but it has yet to evolve into a viable tool for golf courses that need help today. Plant the seeds today, and you will see your investment pay off but in most cases (not all); it will be a slow process so be patient.

8. E-mail marketing: E-mail marketing is probably the most misunderstood and grossly abused golf-marketing platform of all. E-mail marketing is often presented as the best way to market your golf course because it is the most effective and least expensive marketing tool available. This couldn't be further from the truth.

Just as with any other form of marketing, the most important factor is your prospect list. Some golf courses are just now (twenty-five years later than they should have been) building their e-mail lists. Most golf courses have only a handful of e-mail addresses, primarily from current golfers. So most golf-course marketing done via e-mail is actually marketing to the existing membership base made up of core golfers; hence, e-mail marketing does not capture new business in most cases.

E-mail marketing pros: E-mail marketing is affordable or free; the response from your targeted audience is often fast. The customer-tracking ability is great, e-mail-marketing campaigns can be launched with ease, and no other delivery system is faster than e-mail. You have the ability to send different e-mails whenever you wish, reaching targeted audiences by customizing e-mail offers based on their interests.

E-mail marketing cons: E-mail marketing is plagued with security and privacy issues. Most clients nowadays have ad-blocking software, most e-mail ads require customers to download a JPEG or PDF file, and some of these ads are large and, therefore, time-consuming to download. E-mails are sometimes considered unimportant and are often deleted by the audience. Some e-mail ads are hard to read, especially on mobile devices.

Golf course e-marketing is absolutely no to low cost once you have built a database of qualified recipients because the delivery of your message is free. But if you are not building your list, you are not growing your list and, therefore, you are not growing your business. Building a qualified-prospect e-mail list is time-consuming and will require a financial investment. Never buy an e-mail list because it will cause you unmentionable problems with your IP (Internet-protocol) address; your ISP (Internet service provider); your ranking on search engines such as Google, Bing, Yahoo; and so on. Sending out e-mails to a bad list could even get your website blocked or blacklisted.

E-mail marketing is an opt-in form of golf-course marketing, so you must build your list in-house. There are no shortcuts to this process, no matter what anyone tries to tell (or sell) you. Even some of the people who have been in the golf-course–cybermarketing business for years will neglect to tell you the downside to e-marketing just to get you to buy their e-mail-marketing packages. Not everyone will get caught, but for the few who do, it can be devastating.

The CAN-SPAM Act is a law that sets the rules for commercial e-mail, establishes requirements for commercial messages, gives recipients the right to have you stop e-mailing them, and spells out tough penalties for violations.

Here are the penalties for violating the CAN-SPAM Act: Each separate e-mail in violation of the law is subject to penalties of up to *$16,000*, and more than one person may be held responsible for violations. For example, both the company whose product is promoted in the message and the company that originated the message may be legally responsible. E-mails that make misleading claims about products or services also may be subject to laws outlawing deceptive advertising, such as section 5 of the FTC Act. The CAN-SPAM Act has certain aggravated violations that may give rise to additional fines. The law provides for criminal penalties, including imprisonment.

If you buy e-mails from a third party and send them out or have a third party send them out, you are promoting, at your own risk, your products or services to purchased e-mail addresses that have not opted in, but you have been warned. Besides the legalities, it's considered unethical in the cyber world.

9. SMS messages: SMS is a fantastic platform for marketing golf products and services, but this platform is also far from inexpensive. SMS messaging is inexpensive to deliver if it is being sent from an in-house account but can be very expensive if controlled by a third party. It also can be extremely expensive to build your SMS list. SMS marketing in relative terms can be either extremely expensive or inexpensive, depending on whether you are starting with a qualified list of mobile numbers.

If you do not have a qualified list to start with, you must first launch an initial marketing campaign via radio, print, direct mail, and so on just to build the list of mobile phone numbers you'll need for an SMS marketing campaign. SMS marketing is an opt-in form of marketing, so you must get the prospects' permission before messaging them. SMS marketing also demands you keep your messages short and sweet. This requires expert knowledge of golf-marketing psychology.

With that said, SMS is absolutely a great support platform for your marketing campaigns, and if you are smart, you will start capturing mobile numbers immediately, so that when the time comes for you to launch an SMS marketing campaign, you will be prepared. Everything is being condensed to fit on mobile devices, so be prepared to keep your messages to the point. One day in the near future, it will be an excellent way to engage prospects, but for now, it is dependent on other media to first capture golfers' pertinent information and permission.

10. Content marketing: You must design a professional website where you give free information to the public about golf every week. Send out free newsletters (not sales brochures) and articles that give instruction and education on the game. You can also send out free surveys, free data, and so on. Informational and educational content is today's way of selling. The information highway is exactly that—a highway for information to travel on. Consumers have become accustomed to using the Internet to research golf courses, products, and services. Providing premium content is an excellent way to start conversations and relationships with prospects and golfers.

Another method for content marketing would be to put something of great value, such as a free download, on your website as a reward to anyone who registers and then take those who register to a second step of the sales process, which could be having them read your blogs, and so on. Take people through a sales presentation without emphasizing sales. It is your job to engage consumers and keep them engaged with valuable content. Freebies and bonuses are also excellent ways of doing this. Show your visitors you are just as interested in serving as you are in selling.

11. Flyers: Most of us just starting out can't afford to pay for direct mail, but we can photocopy flyers and put them in mailboxes around our neighborhood. Make it fun, and incorporate it into your exercise regimen. Walk and put out flyers for an hour every day. There are companies that specialize in this business of putting out door hangers. They hire people for minimum wage to hang advertising on doorknobs. If you can't afford to pay for advertising, get out and start walking.

12. Mail-outs: Birthday cards, Christmas cards, motivational postcards, invitational letters, and so on are all great ways to follow up with prospects you have just spoken with over the phone or met briefly. Everyone wants (and needs) to feel special, whether he or she will admit it or not, and tangible correspondence meets this need far better than an e-mail or other digital communication; mail-outs are a great way to stay connected. Remember in the sales presentation when I discussed the four different social styles: the director, the analytic, the socialist, and the relator? Your prospect's dominant social style and preferred communication method will dictate your follow-up strategy. With directors, who are concerned only with the bottom line in the beginning, you do not want to call them all the time to follow up because they will inevitably get annoyed with your interruptions and blow you off for good. Handwritten (legible) cards are perfect for this scenario along with occasional follow-up calls. On the other hand, if your prospect is a socialist, a phone call would be expected, but a handwritten note on a card would be cherished. Socialists love the connection and look forward to and welcome new relationships. A relator will need a list of testimonials, and an analytic will want all the details in writing that can be followed up with a card or handwritten note. People like people like themselves; do not forget this fact, and follow the prospect's style of preferred communication, not yours.

If you are just fishing for prospects and have not spent enough time with someone to determine his or her preferred style of communication or social style, then use the shotgun method until you find what works best. Always keep a budget for mail-outs. You have an exact bull's-eye on qualified prospects; it's personal, tangible, and direct.

Again, set your goals with your desired outcome; do your homework; design your presentation pieces and ad copy; decide on your hook; and go for it!

I have just given you a dozen low-cost ways to bring in new business. You don't have to use them all (although you should), but even if you use just a few, you will have a few more opportunities every day to get a golfer committed to your course. One of my favorite sayings is "Luck is when preparation meets opportunity." Always be prepared and ABP.

Golf-course marketing and professional golf membership sales go hand in hand. One of the things the sales community talks about the most is leads. Whether they are cold or hot, qualified or not, the bottom line is if you have a warm body with the money to join your course, you have a smokin' hot sales lead. I have never looked at prospects in front of me, referrals from my golfers, or guests who are brought in by a golfer to play a round as my only hot leads. Don't take what I am saying the wrong way; those referrals and walk-ins definitely qualify as hot leads. But buddy referrals and walk-ins are not your only source of hot leads. Just think about it: everybody in your community is theoretically a hot lead, so go out and get 'em to come take a tour of your magnificent golf course.

If it is your responsibility to grow the business, you must grow the business immediately. Start by getting a list of all the businesses in your area, put together a corporate membership offer, and get it in the decision maker's hand. Partner with your local chamber of commerce, and get them to send an e-mail to all their members. Contact local high schools, colleges, fire departments, police stations, and on and on. If you are the golf pro, then set up some free clinics and advertise them through social media and on your course's website. Yes, it will require some time and work, but if growing the business is your job, you need to be doing it well. Just for the record, if part of your job is to grow the business, then yes, sales, lead generation, and marketing are in your job description.

You have now been given a dozen low- to no-cost ways to market your course and generate leads; there are no excuses now. Perfect using these tools, and soon marketing budgets won't be a problem. Most owners have no idea of the importance of marketing and advertising because when they have been dragged kicking and screaming to spend the money on advertising, the campaigns usually flopped back in in their faces like a duffed sand wedge out of a bunker. They say the proof is in the pudding, so it is your job to give the owner a little taste of how successful you can grow the business with little to no budget. If you do, I assure you he or she will be more than willing to make future investments into marketing and advertising.

CHAPTER 4

THE LONG GAME: PUTTING ALL THE PIECES TOGETHER

My goal after entering the golf industry was to identify, engage, and lock up relationships with the difficult-to-reach segments of consumers who have purchased within the golf category but may or may not have ever played the game, that is, the casual and nongolfers. Subconsciously, I had been preparing for this day my entire life; I even named my company Mulligan Marketing Concepts fifteen years before I launched my first campaign for a golf course. I had studied every facet of identifying, engaging, and locking up relationships with untapped segments since my first days in the health-club industry back in 1982. I was a sponge that absorbed every ounce of pertinent information relative to increasing revenue and sales. For a decade and a half, I had been raising hundreds of thousands of dollars a month for more than five hundred privately owned and operated health clubs, and now I was going to apply all I knew about identifying, engaging, and locking up relationships with members that came from an untapped demographic to the golf industry. I knew I could create a product that would carry a golf course for two to three years, which would be long enough for the owners and management to cultivate relationships with the new golfers and earn their long-term loyalty.

I first needed to do my research. The first place everyone should start when building a business or launching a new product is research. I knew I had to target a much larger demographic/segment than what was currently being addressed because there are not enough avid and core golfers in most markets to keep all the courses in business, much less profitable. From experience, it was crystal clear to me that no one was tapping into these new segments because no one knew how to identify who they were or, even harder, how to get them in the door. Most people who buy golf courses normally have an emotional tie with the game but very little working knowledge of the business. They include doctors, lawyers, athletes, industry people, investors, real-estate developers, city officials, or people who love the game of golf who have an aha moment and think, I should build or buy a golf course.

It is the entrepreneurs' love for the game and lifestyle that blinds them from the reality—and in some cases the nightmare—of running a golf course–like a business. That is, of course, until their entire life savings have been depleted, their business is underwater, and the bank won't float them any more loans. Up until then, they suffer from the Field of Dreams delusion: build it, and they shall come. Had they done only the most basic research, they would have known that less than 10 percent of the US population are "golfers." The data will tell you anywhere between 7 and 9 percent of the population play golf on a regular basis, which is made up of core and avid golfers. The typical data also shows another 1–2 percent have an interest in golf—casual golfers. This is where MMC®'s data and real-world experience differ from conventional data. We have found the casual segment to be much higher. MMC®'s research shows it to be more than 10 percent; that is, there are more casual golfers than core and avid golfers. Of course, this segment plays very few rounds per year and in many cases only one round per year, making them difficult to count. Most companies compiling this data look at casual golfers as those who golf eight to twelve rounds per year. I, on the other hand, believe if a consumer swings a golf club on a course even once a year, he or she is a casual golfer and, therefore, a hot lead or potential target. This segment is one of the two overlooked segments that could be and should be the icing on the cake for golf courses and entrepreneurs. The other segment is the nongolfer—the consumer who has purchased within the golf category but has yet to be identified or engaged by the golf industry.

Up until recently, you never heard the term (label) *nongolfer*, not until MMC® entered the picture. I always look for the segments of "consumers" who have been passed up or neglected because that is where the real money is always buried. These segments are always difficult to identify, engage, and lock up relationships with, so most marketers avoid them, choosing the path of least resistance. In addition to those three segments previously mentioned (core, avid, and casual) that most industry people are familiar with, we have now discovered a new segment that we have labeled nongolfers. This segment has purchased within the golf category—merchandise, apparel, equipment, subscriptions, and so on, which counts for an additional 10 percent of the population. It is the casual and nongolfer segments where MMC® focuses its marketing efforts. This segment adds an additional 10 percent to the target market. In short, MMC® targets the 20 percent of the market that all other golf courses and golf-marketing companies overlook because all they know is the *golfer* demographic.

Here is a quick formula you can use to see whether you should open a golf course in a given county, town, or city. Please keep in mind that there are many factors that must be considered; use this simple matrix as just a starting point to measure whether or not it is even worthwhile to pursue the project. Put your proposed location in Google Maps and draw a twenty- to thirty-mile circle around it. Do not BS yourself; accurately determine how far people will drive to play a round of golf in your geographical area. The travel time should be no longer than thirty to forty-five minutes. I am not factoring in destination play, just local golfers.

Next, look at the number of households (not number of people), and take 8 percent of that number, and you will have a calculated guess as to the number of potential core and avid golfers that a course can draw from your geographical area. Then take the number of golf facilities within that circle, and draw the same circle around those courses. Subtract the appropriate households based on the overlapping properties, and divide that number equally, for example, if a competitor's course's circle falls in the southeast portion of your circle, and there are five thousand households in that area. Subtract half of those households (twenty-five hundred) from your total.

Let me address two things at this point: why I look at households and not population and why I say 8 percent and not 20 or 30 percent. When gathering data it is important to understand why grouping is important. As a group, consumers do predictable things that can be easily measured whereas it is very difficult and costly to measure the individual, so for preliminary data I prefer to count households and not population. Next, I use 8 percent because other than MMC® no one knows how to capture the casual and nongolfers, so stick with numbers and demographics you know—the avid and core golfer. You and every other golf-course business in that radius will be competing for that 8 percent, so do not be fooled, as so many before you have been, by thinking the little nine-hole down the street is not competition. If it has even one person giving it business as little as one dollar, it is your competition, because that one body came from the 8 percent.

I have been conducting health-club research since the mid-1980s and golf-course research since the mid-1990s. I always prefer to err on the conservative side, so with my formula, you might be happily surprised but not devastated by overinflated hope and unrealistic numbers. Of course, there are bonus golfers like those golfers who drive by your course on their way to and from work or who live a little farther out, but do not factor these prospects into your equation. This matrix will give you some insight whether to pursue the venture or to walk away.

Learn everything you can about every private, public, semiprivate, muni, nine-hole, resort property, driving range, and so on within that market, and go visit them all. Ask them questions about their membership, their membership rates, green fees, and cart fees; sit through and actively listen to their sales presentation; go back several times—especially on Saturday and Sunday mornings between 6:00 a.m. and 11:00 a.m.—and look at their parking lots to see how crowded they are. Play a round as a guest, and ask some of the staff how many golfers they have. You can even try to guess (because that is all you can really do at this stage of your research) how many golfers each course has based on their tee-sheet (available tee-times) and how many cars are in the parking lot each day if you can't get a number from one of the staff.

The golf business is all about the numbers, and most mainstream data reports core golfers golf fifty to a hundred times a year, avid golfers twenty-five to fifty times a year, and casual golfers eight to twelve rounds per year. These numbers are based on averages from across the United

States and will vary from course to course and in regard to the organizations gathering the data, but they are close enough for you to gauge the feasibility of opening a course in the market you have chosen as a start-up business with limited resources. At least, you'll be able to make some educated guesses. Do not factor in the casual and nongolfer segments because you do not have the resources to identify, engage, and lock up those relationships. Stick with what you know—the core and avid golfers.

Take your 8 percent of households, which will give you your potential market and then subtract the overlapping households as well as the possible golfers enrolled with your competition. Remove them from your total, and now you have a realistic number of potential golfers for your course and the number of rounds you can expect to host as well as an idea of the potential revenue. Keep in mind that I haven't discussed all the variables that could catapult your revenue far beyond the norm: for example, you own a niche portion of the market; your service is unparalleled; you are the most convenient; your amenities blow the competition's away; you have a top-notch, well-trained membership-sales staff using a professional sales system; your marketing company works twenty-four hours a day, seven days a week, promoting your golf course as well as your golf products and services; and so on. I am just talking hard, raw basic numbers.

I too wanted to research my targeted audience before I ever attempted to approach a golf-course owner about running a campaign. I had seen endless owners struggle with their marketing, and in my opinion, it was mostly because of their worn-out and misdirected ads. They went after the same market their competitors had gone after—the core and avid golfers with the same ads. Everyone was seeing the same ads with the same offers all the time. I knew if I was going to be successful, I would have to build a consumer profile of my clients' ideal customer, and that is exactly what I did.

We started our research the old-fashioned way: by talking to golfers and nongolfers alike. By talking to your existing golfers you can gather some of the best free information, education, and data not available through conventional sources. The research I am referring to is called primary research. Primary research is custom- designed (by yourself or a company you hire) for the particular needs of a company like MMC®

to profile the ideal customer for their clients, or a company like yours to improve your services and grow your business, but is often conducted by professional researchers.

In today's world of the Internet, the research can also be done by layman if they have the time to devote to learning the craft. This is necessary research if you plan on growing your business or career, especially as a marketer. I will discuss in some detail the process I used, while explaining some of the end results I was looking for, so that you too may apply some of the same techniques to your business's research.

First, you need to think of research in two ways:

1.   Golfers' attitudes—emotions and feelings
2.   Golfers' behaviors—buying patterns and spending habits

You start primary research by listening to your golfers and not yourself. Suspend your ego temporarily, and get the information you need from the source—your golfers. Your golfers have a wealth of information just waiting to be harvested. They will tell you why they are happy, sad, disappointed, and pleased; why they joined; why they didn't join your competitor; why they stay; or worse, why they are planning to leave.

In my case, my team and I interviewed hundreds of golfers and non-golfers alike. I wanted to know why certain people loved being members of their local golf course, yet others never joined. What were their fears, what media caught their attention, what they read or just tossed, what programs they watched, what made them flip the channel, what were the psychological triggers that had made them not buy, and what were the triggers that had made them buy? Many marketers miss the boat when it comes to demographic research because they focus primarily on income and age—which are two of the most basic qualifiers that fall at the very bottom of a comprehensive consumer profile. Keep in mind that when golfers (consumers) are asked questions about a product or service, their knee-jerk response is normally price. When digging a little deeper during a personal one-on-one interview or small-group setting, you'll find that this isn't always the real challenge that must be addressed and overcome. If you ask some simple questions, you will uncover unmet needs, wants, wishes, and desires and then you can design a way to identify those consumers as a group. The realities of the marketplace can force you to rethink your position and priorities, so you must know your target audience like the back of your hand before launching a new product.

Today, there is a ton of information readily available via the Internet. There has been a global explosion of consumer-behavior information available to anyone who is willing to invest the time and personnel to find it. Massive databases allow marketers access to credit-card spending patterns; consumers' purchase habits; and demographic data that is even broken down by zip codes, neighborhoods, and street addresses. You (anyone with the time, a clear objective, and Internet access) can also unearth or purchase data about golfers from numerous sources on the Internet, which are not easily surrendered by participants who take part in surveys or focus groups. Some of this information is even free. The process of gathering the data and interpreting the information is time consuming, but if you have more time than money, it is definitely an option.

Market research has always been at the top of my list and is now MMC®'s top priority. When I was building this company, and even during its inception, my focus was on the member. Throughout this book, I use the term win-win; this is the guiding principle of my life. If golfers can feel like winners by joining my clients' golf courses as opposed to their competitors', they will feel more connected to the courses, which in turn will inspire member loyalty. This philosophy creates the ultimate win-win relationship, so I took my research a lot deeper than I had first anticipated, before I had ever considered launching this new-golfer-acquisition campaign.

My goal was, and still is, to define our client's target audience on a national scale, so we dug deeper and deeper to unearth as much applicable information as possible. We researched consumers' psychographics, including attitudes, beliefs, perceptions, lifestyles, personality traits, frequencies of purchase, frequencies of product or service use within the golfer categories, volume of purchases, rates of use, occasions of use, brand loyalties, price sensitivities, price levels, buying situations or occasions, demographics, geographic areas, and on and on.

I contracted many people and companies to help with this process, and this research is still ongoing even today. MMC®'s team of researchers is gathering new data daily for all our clients. Any given project has up to thirty people devoted to its success. In the late 1980s, I had to purchase all this data from outside sources, and through decades of experience and hundreds of thousands of dollars invested, I eventually learned how to conduct more detailed research specific to MMC®'s golf-marketing needs so that later in my career, when I could afford it, I built a research center where we have employed an entire department that works twenty-four hours a day, seven days a week, gathering and interpreting data for our clients. After profiling my ideal target, I needed to design ad copy that focused on getting targets (prospects and guests) through the door. I set out to accomplish this through perfecting my message and offer.

It's important to understand psychology as it relates to selling golf memberships, golf products, and services. Knowing the needs and wants of your audience and how your golf product can satisfy them is critical to your success. You might golf because it makes you feel successful. Some people golf because it allows them to connect with their friends; others because it helps them build new relationships or rekindle old relationships; some because the game is challenging, and they are excited to see the improvements in their game; and some because golfing makes them feel good. Never be fooled into believing your golfers join for the same reasons. There are, however, a core set of reasons or emotions that can explain 80 percent of your golfers' buying decisions.

You must know what emotion(s) the customer in front of you is chasing so that you can let him or her experience that feeling right then, which will start the process of him or her linking extreme pleasure to your product or service. Try to think about the value of your brand in terms of its emotional equity—how your golf course, product, or service makes your prospects and golfers feel. The biggest mistake we can make is to think every guest or golfer comes through our door for the same reason(s) or is interested in our product or service for the same reason(s) we are.

Part of MMC®'s focus is on meeting the six core emotional needs of the consumer in our advertising as well as in our sales presentations. Security, importance, excitement, connection, growth, and contribution are all emotions that must be connected with your golf product or service and conveyed through your marketing and sales systems. Once I knew my target (the casual and nongolfers) market, I had to design my advertising to trigger their core emotional needs.

I know some owners hate having memberships because they feel the "member" is beating the system, and they are correct; core and avid members do beat the system. Let's face it: these golfers get out their calculators and punch in the number of rounds they play and divide it by the membership rate. If they come out better with a membership, then they'll buy a membership, and if they don't, then they don't. This is one of the main reasons I stress golf courses need a balance of core, avid, casual, and nongolfers. Most core golfers play golf for under ten dollars per round when you do the math, but that's OK because owners need core golfers' guaranteed annual revenue to pay the bills, and if you want to enjoy the benefits of consumer loyalty, you must have a membership model.

Here are some numbers you must know if you own a golf course:

The following is a sample breakdown of a property hosting twenty thousand rounds during a thirty-week season and how those rounds are divided among core, avid, and casual golfers. Keep in mind that the actual numbers may differ (hopefully, they differ a lot) from course to course, but the percentages are pretty consistent.

Just to be clear, 26,500 rounds is a good break-even number (average) for most golf properties with a thirty-week season, especially throughout the heart of America, the Midwest. So if you are hosting only twenty thousand rounds, someone is dipping into his own pocket, and you need to call MMC® immediately.

Here is the breakdown:

- 100 core members playing 80 rounds = 8,000
- 40 outings a year x 60 rounds = 2,400 rounds in outing play
- 200 avid golfers playing 30 rounds = 6,000 rounds
- 70 percent core and avid golfers plus 10 percent outing play = 80 percent (16,400 rounds) are being consumed by 40 percent of the golfers
- 360 casual golfers playing 10 rounds = 3,600

- According to the numbers, only 20 percent of the rounds are being consumed by casual golfers
- The only variable is leagues, for example, fifteen hundred to two thousand rounds.

There are only 660 unique bodies consuming the twenty thousand rounds.

If you want to increase rounds and revenue, you must bring in new bodies! You must grow the game to grow your business and your career. The only way to grow the game is to penetrate new segments.

Your goal should be fifty thousand rounds for a thirty-week season. Why? Because even in goal setting, the 80/20 rule applies. If you reach only 80 percent of your goal, you'll at least be hosting forty thousand rounds.

The goal is to increase the number of casual golfers and interject nongolfers because avid and core golfers know the ins and outs of spending the least amount of money while getting the most value. The key to golf marketing and sales is to find the win-win balance of giving the prospects enough value to get them committed without giving them too much value relative to their investment. But how much is enough and not too much? I knew the only way I was going to find the answer to that question was through experience (trial and error) and more research.

To be successful in marketing and sales, I had to learn the negative and positive emotions prospects associated with golf and joining a loyalty program. Then I needed to find ways to replace the negative associations with positive associations. For example, I needed to exchange fear with excitement, frustration with growth, worry with security, regret with connection, embarrassment with contribution, hopelessness with significance, and so on. I knew this process could start with proper ad copy and design. My goal was to get prospects to link positive emotions to my clients' products, no matter what their reputations in the marketplace had been, good or bad. My campaigns needed to raise immediate cash and long-term revenue, but they also needed to build the course's brand within the community.

Let's take a moment now to discuss what other kinds of studies have been done on behalf of MMC® for the golf industry. Focus groups are one of the top ways to determine whether a product, service, business concept, and so on is appealing to the public and why or why not. We also gathered valuable feedback via detailed questionnaires to help build a profile of the ideal prospect. We were able to discern what the consumers liked or disliked about every microscopic detail of the golf products and services. This data gave me a wealth of information.

Observation studies also were incorporated into our research to help identify how consumers viewed golf memberships and loyalty programs. We conducted the studies in a relaxed one-on-one setting, and they produced valuable insights into the thoughts of potential golfers and customers. Mall interception with shoppers and personal interviews conducted in homes were also used to gather relevant information to help with the casual and nongolfer profiles. Research is about asking consumers how they feel about products and services. During our interviews, my team and I uncovered important attitudes, perceptions, beliefs, and behaviors that proved invaluable when it came to building the profiles.

Massive databases allow marketers such as MMC® to access critical information such as credit-card spending patterns, consumers' purchase habits, and demographic data that enable us to target the preferred demographic. Capturing customer information like this ensures business growth and prevents wasteful spending. This approach allows us to allocate marketing dollars more effectively. We are in an era of exploding information, and I was determined to put MMC® at the forefront of the golf-course industry when it came to acquiring new golfers using up-to-date data. Of course, being able to gather a lot of this information via the Internet came much, much later for me and MMC®, but it would be remiss of me if I did not share this information with you in this book.

If you have the time or manpower available, much research information can be found absolutely free. Many local and federal institutions conduct research and surveys every minute of the day, most of which can be found on the Internet. Just enter your search words and phrases into any search engine, and you'll be on your way. Another great source is trade publications and organizations, but remember that they too are in business to make money, so do your homework. Don't forget your local library, which is another great resource. Libraries have entire sections devoted to research (which may not be found in electronic formats) and provide a staff to assist you in finding things fast. Some of these surveys are conducted through the Internet, over the telephone, through snail mail, through personal interviews, and so on, but no matter how, when, or why the information was gathered, it will serve as a valuable resource throughout your career.

Some of the things I had hoped to achieve from my research included becoming aware of consumers' perceptions of golf courses within a given market and learning the likes and dislikes of past, current, and potential golfers. I wanted to hear suggestions and ideas that could enhance services and products and listen to stories, both good and bad, about people's experiences with golf courses. I wanted to uncover patterns of behavior, learn about the decision-making processes, and find out who was involved in those processes: spouses, family members, and friends. In short, I wanted to learn how to identify and engage the casual and nongolfers.

Profiling gives you a much greater chance of knowing where and how to focus your marketing efforts, thereby avoiding wasteful spending while increasing the return on your investment. With this information, I would be able to implement customer-penetration programs and bring in new business from untapped segments of the market. This wasn't just about being better than my competitors, this was about the long game— this was about growing the game.

I relied on both qualitative and quantitative studies to profile the targeted market. Qualitative studies include focus groups, mini-focus groups, dyads, triads, in-depth personal interviews, observational studies, and brainstorming sessions, to name just a few. Quantitative studies include segmentation studies, communication studies, advertising-execution studies, advertising-awareness and tracking studies, price studies, and customer-satisfaction research.

My team and I also wanted to understand both strategic research, which helped determine the most promising and profitable courses of action, and tactical strategies, which helped determine how best to pursue those courses of action in relation to my marketing campaigns.

Now that I had a detailed profile of my target and knew the message I wanted to convey, it was time to find the best form of marketing, advertising, or promotional materials and media to use to engage the profiled targets. I did a ton of research on this subject as well: communication studies, advertising-execution studies, advertising-awareness studies, tracking studies, and packaging studies were all part of the research that led me eventually to settle on print advertisement as the driving force of my campaigns. I realize this seems overwhelming and, quite frankly, it is. When I first started this journey, I had no idea of the amount of information, education, and data that was needed to successfully penetrate an untapped market.

I was determined to design a campaign with a customer-penetration strategy that could not fail, and I was willing to study anything and everything possible to accomplish this goal. Today, MMC®'s research department constantly monitors digital conversations via blogs; chat rooms; e-mails; and social networks such as FB, Myspace, LinkedIn, and Twitter, where customers are talking about the golf industry. These digital conversations contain real-time, pertinent information for acquiring desirable targets. This is just one way MMC® has grown over the years, helping our clients develop a competitive advantage in their markets.

I was also aware that I must discover the very best delivery system for my message, so I studied direct mail, website-content development, e-marketing campaigns, radio, television, and so on. Don't be naïve; marketing and advertising are necessary to increase the level of awareness in your community, and if you want to grow your business, you better study all available resources.

In MMC®'s infancy, there were no free platforms such as websites, social media, and e-marketing. These new platforms needed to be studied as they hit the marketplace and started grabbing traction. Although I am not a tech guy by any stretch of the imagination, I learned a long time ago to "hire for the position." I hired people who were not only qualified for the job but also loved the job they were being hired to do. As marketing started becoming more successful in the digital world, I assembled a team of IT professionals to maximize MMC®'s proficiency in the electronic world. But in the beginning of my career, I had to learn how to maximize the ROI from traditional media such as radio, newspaper, direct mail, and television ads; these were the four staples when it came to getting your message out. The great thing about studying these traditional media is that the education I earned is still paying off today when working with other media and platforms. There are far more resources readily available to you in 2017 than there were in the mid-1980s and 1990s when I first started this research, so get off your couch and start studying!

The only way to learn the most effective media is through trial and error. I was and still am very fortunate in this area because I work with numerous clients in every geographical area imaginable and have the flexibility to test new ideas at will because I am bringing in a ton of revenue; most courses and even fewer marketers have this luxury. As I said earlier, different media target, different demographics. For example, if I am targeting the hero generation and some of the baby boomers, we might focus on newspaper or radio. If we are targeting Generation X as well as baby boomers, we might focus on direct mail along with some e-marketing and radio. If we are targeting millennials, we will focus on social media, e-marketing, and SMS as well as direct mail. But if we have the money, we will always use direct mail as the driving force of the campaign because, hands down, it yields the greatest ROI. I always say we may focus on a certain media, but this is not a set rule. Every project is completely unique, and you must do your research on a case-by-case basis before launching the campaign because the bottom line…is the bottom line.

Back in the day, everyone wanted to run television ads, but TV commercials are really feasible only for owners of multiple properties. When you are running a single golf course, for example, television commercials are probably one of the worst investments for growing your golf course (but they do a lot for your ego), due to the wide geographical area that television serves. On the other hand, because the reach is so vast, if you have multiple locations, the commercials can yield a decent return. Of course, this is only if you have the money to run multiple commercials to make the imprint necessary to get your brand fixed in the viewers' minds, which demands repetitive ads and even more repetition to get viewers to take action. TV commercials have the ability to capture the complete attention of your prospect because you can be creative in your ads through images and sound, which are two very important senses. Television stations have real-time tracking ability when it comes to knowing the number of people watching at any given time as well as a rudimentary demographic profile of the viewers. The downside to television advertisement is the creative, production, and airtime costs that make it very expensive, in addition to maintaining scripts, concepts, and designs that can be even more expensive because they all must be rewritten or updated often. Television ads are very short, which requires your ads to be creative enough to get the interest of the audience in just a few seconds, and this also means you are very limited in your message. Studies also show that, in many cases, people do not believe the ads they see on TV. Other challenges are that customers tend to do something else during commercial breaks, and most importantly, viewers lack station loyalty, which may require you to advertise on more than one station to get the desired results.

Radio is still (as of 2017) a reliable source of getting the message out, especially for generational marketing, although the demographic profile is also elementary at best. The key to this media is that you must make sure you can convey your message with a call-to-action in a thirty- or sixty-second spot. Radio engages the auditory senses, so maximize that aspect of your message by being creative with sounds and music. As I discussed earlier, you must get the customer's senses involved, and radio is a great way to achieve this goal. Think about the mood you are looking to set and then get the music that will move your listeners toward that mood. Radio is still a good support media for a marketing campaign because it is cost effective and easy to produce. There are a few negatives, such as the geographical area it covers, which probably goes far beyond your business's reach. Yes, 5, 10, or 20 percent of your golfers will come from outside your target market, but their numbers are very low relative to the overall pool of prospects. So targeting a larger market in most cases is a waste of money, but with radio being so affordable in most markets, I am able to reach enough prospects within the target market to justify the enlarged market reach of the station.

Some of the negatives you hear about radio advertisement are the following: short exposure due to thirty- or sixty-second spots, so just like television, you must do repetitive ads so that you'll stick in the listener's mind; limited time equates to limited content; there is a lack of trackability for ad-success rate (although I disagree with this—we at MMC® teach our clients' staff to ask every prospect how he or she heard about the course); there is a lack of visual perception from the audience, which makes it hard to remember because the prospect cannot go back to review important details (this is why I couple radio with some print ads); in some cases, radio is considered background noise and does not have a focused audience; ads are sometimes considered an unwelcome interruption of the music, and listeners often switch stations to avoid listening to advertisements; there is no tangible reference for residual effect; radio is notorious for ad clutter (one ad after another); and you must advertise on more than one station simultaneously to reach different demographics. Bottom line: I am a fan of radio despite its negatives, but again, only as a support media and only when I am targeting a specific demographic.

Another media I use to deliver my message is print ads. I often use them when targeting specific demographic groups with an emphasis on certain generations. With print ads, you can say a lot in a small space. A picture can speak a thousand words, and this is even truer when it comes to print ads. I am a fan of advertising in newspapers (although the core audience is dying off), especially when the ad space can be bartered out. Whether you pay for the ads or barter for them, always make sure you get online ads to support your marketing campaigns. Newspapers allow you to reach a large number of people in a given geographical area, and subscribers are normally loyal customers. You must know the demographic you are trying to reach. Older generations are more likely to read the newspaper as a habit, whereas millennials tend to get their news from online platforms.

Another advantage of advertising in newspapers is the different ad sizes available. This allows you to advertise within your budget. Advertisers will tell you that people also have been known to keep and read newspapers for a few days as well as share them with others, which increases your visibility, although in reality, newspapers are more than likely read once or twice on average. The key to success is to make your ads stand out from the clutter of other ads on a page. Try to place your ads in the top-right corner of the right page; this is the place where your readers will be most likely to notice your ad. Newspaper ads can be expensive since multiple insertions are necessary to make an impact, so do your homework. The biggest downside of newspaper ads is the demographic they reach, which is primarily the older generations, and with the explosion of the Internet, there has been a huge decline in newspaper readership.

Direct mail is my preference above all other media. When I first started selling clubs on my Cash campaign, I ran into continuous push-back because of the cost, but I understood the cost was the only true negative for direct mail. If managed properly, direct mail can actually be self-funding. It is an absolute must to partner with a vendor who is up to date on the latest requirements of the postal service, so that the mailing house can do all the presorting and handling of the mail to get the very best postal rates and preferred time of delivery for clients.

I studied all forms of media but could not get any one of them to perform as well as profiled, personalized direct mail. Direct mail is highly selective and specifically targets the desired market; it allows me to be creative through visual aids; it lands in the hands of 99.9 percent of the prospects on my mailing list; it yields the highest ROI; I can include unlimited content relative to the piece; it is very easy to track the audience's response; it is cost-effective relative to the ROI; it's tangible; it involves essential sensory participation from a person; and most importantly, it allows our clients to build an enormous in-house database for future campaigns. There is only one challenge with direct mail, and that is cost. That is why I had to design my campaigns to be completely (100 percent) self-funding from the very beginning.

If you are a marketer, you must reverse any risk to the customer and sell the result of the product or service. So, when trying to acquire clients, you must show them there is zero downside and the result will solve at least one of—but hopefully most of—their problems. I am a staunch believer in direct mail (if done correctly) because of the immediate and long-term residual effects a business receives, including but not limited to branding and residual sales revenue.

Businesspeople want to know the ROI or the return they'll receive on their marketing dollars. I live, eat, and breathe marketing and sales, so I have a more aggressive attitude to monies spent on marketing than most, but any businessperson knows numbers, and numbers never lie. I think if you are getting an ROI of 10 percent or better, you should keep doing what you are doing, because you're extremely lucky to get that rate of return from any investment. I have frequently seen ROIs from MMC®'s direct-mail campaigns yield 100–500 percent; for MMC®, a 100 percent ROI is on the low side. You'll get that kind of return only once in a lifetime, if then, from any other legitimate investment.

It baffles me when owners complain about the cost of direct mail when they are getting a 100 or even 200 percent return. If they just thought of their other investments—such as stocks, bonds, and CDs, which get 3–15 percent—they might gain a little perspective. Traditional investments take years to see a return, and with direct mail, the return is immediate as well as long term. There is absolutely no better investment in business. Besides, I'll invest in my own capabilities before I turn my money over to some fund manager who gets paid win or lose.

Direct mail has numerous advantages over all other media. As I stated earlier, with direct mail you can write an article, a book, or as much as you want, although you always want to keep your ad copy short and sweet. You could also put an insert into your direct-mail piece that gives more detailed information, such as a DVD or a flash drive. With direct mail, you are reaching the most qualified prospects available in your target market. You must also consider your geographic target market, which could be up to a twenty or thirty-mile radius around your golf course, depending on the drive time. Direct-mail campaigns are sniper campaigns, with each individual qualified prospect in your crosshairs.

When you enlist direct mail as the driving force of your marketing strategy, you can target people through a profiled mailing list using demographic and psychographic data that will help you eliminate wasteful spending and yield a higher ROI. Direct mail is absolutely the best delivery system to capture and acquire the most qualified golfers—those consumers within your geographical reach that have disposable incomes.

Since you have no limit on content other than the size of your piece, you can convey a detailed message. It is easy to track your audience's response effectively with direct mail; costs are controlled by you and your budget; you have full control over creativity and execution from start to stamp, and every piece is personalized and addressed to the recipient (at least, that is how MMC® does direct mail). Direct mail is the most engaging of all advertising, and the impact of direct mail goes far beyond the immediate returns. Direct mail's residual effect brings customers in for months and years to come. It is very hard for your competitors to track and copy direct mail until you release the mail, which makes copying your pieces a losing proposition.

When it comes to direct mail, volume speaks volumes. Direct mail should be deployed in volume. You must target every "qualified" prospect in your market and get your course in front of him or her often. Business is a numbers game, and direct mail is a numbers game. When it comes to profiling casual and nongolfers through demographics and psychographics, there is no better marketing strategy available than purchasing or renting quality lists based on the prospects' buying patterns and spending habits as well as their geographic locations relative to the golf course. Don't waste marketing dollars on undesirable targets; put your message in the hands of golfers you would be proud to call members and loyal customers.

Every owner wants to get the biggest bang for his or her buck from marketing. Direct mail does just that; not only is it a huge revenue producer when designed correctly, but it also gives the course enormous exposure in the right places, which is in their immediate areas. Golf-course exposure is just one of the reasons I choose to use direct mail as the driving force of our campaigns. Direct mail also gives the golf course the most exposure from the least investment.

Golf-marketing exposure means you get your brand in front of as many golfers as possible. This can be done effectively only through direct mail. Most owners have a difficult time understanding the ROI when it comes to direct mail. Direct mail not only gives you the greatest immediate results but also provides the business with long-term residual dividends paid through brand recognition and future sales.

Another reason I love direct mail is that it allows you to repeat the message over and over to pique the prospects' interest, and by doing so, it will start to condition golfers to think of your golf course when they think of golf. The only thing better than direct mail would be to go to each "qualified" house in your market, knock on the door, and introduce your golf course with a PowerPoint presentation. But even then, you would still need the pertinent data to profile qualified prospects, or you would just be wasting 80 percent of your time and money knocking on unqualified doors.

I always get a kick out of owners and pros when we are in a meeting discussing marketing concepts and they tell me their best market is a neighborhood thirty or forty minutes away. They normally say this because it is a higher income area, and they want to pull from that area because they fantasize this is their demographic. They will even sometimes say, "I live there and I drive here every day." And I reply, "Well, you drive here every day because you have your entire life savings or credit rating tied up in this place; prospects don't share the same motivation as you." You can absolutely pull those people from there, but it takes a lot more than simple desire. In fact, it takes a lot of know-how and patience, and you must create a need and desire for the golfers to drive the extra distance. But I want to give you tools you can put to use today, right now. So my advice is to focus on your immediate area and price your memberships and green fees based on the demographic makeup of your local market and not on the demographic makeup of your wish list.

One of the most memorable instances in my golf-marketing career thus far was when I first launched MMC®'s golf division in 2006, which we partnered with a course in Georgia to run our Cash campaign. The owner was an older gentleman who had been a golf pro for a hundred years (seemed like) and had built a beautiful course on his wife's family farm. He had spent a fortune on this build-out. The first couple of years, he knocked the cover off the ball (which makes sense because it was new), but then it got harder and harder to get golfers. This guy hated most people including his golfers. He started going under water and decided to call us. I could see he had many challenges, but the biggest was his elitist attitude. He felt that because he had built this beautiful course everyone who stepped foot on the property should pay homage to him for being allowed to pay to play his course. He also made the brilliant decision to hire people who were just like him, which made for an interesting dynamic in the clubhouse. His other challenge was that although his course was beautiful, its surrounding area was lower middle class. When we started the campaign, we informed him we would be focusing our efforts on his local market (a twenty-mile radius around his golf course). He argued and complained throughout the entire campaign, claiming it wasn't his market because all that was there were trailer parks (which was in itself an exaggeration). He insisted his market was thirty-five miles away and that we didn't know his course or area. I assured him we did know and had all the supporting data to prove it. I also pointed out that "trailer park trash" would never make it through our vetting process, so there was no need to worry. To make a long story short, we brought him about fifteen hundred golfers and raised about $300,000 in up-front cash and over $600,000 in back-end revenue. He was shocked at the success (although he never quit complaining), but he was happy nonetheless and wrote us a glowing testimonial.

Price analysis plays an important role in golf marketing, but most golf courses fail to conduct this analysis properly. Most golf courses are raising their membership rates and/or green fees but have no solid research or increased value to substantiate or justify the increase. Between 2000 and 2005, I conducted in-depth research for MMC®'s Cash campaign and exposed the true value and perceived value of golf courses across the country because, in the end, it doesn't really matter what owners, pros, and managers think the value of the membership or green fees are; the only thing that matters is what the market thinks.

I had to identify how much the prospective golfer was willing to pay before I put a price for membership or green fees out into the marketplace. The market may not have the same perceived value of your golf products and services as you do. The perceived value of the owners, pros, and managers is irrelevant to the paying golfer, who will dictate the pricing structure, or at least a portion thereof, whether they like it or not. I see this every day when courses are constantly adjusting their rates to accommodate the golfer. Far too often, golf courses price their memberships and green fees based on their competitors' rates. This is absurd. But the absurdity doesn't stop there either. Some courses price their memberships and green fees out of the market, and others price their memberships and green fees too low—devaluing their own product.

You can't just set your rates for memberships or green fees without conducting some fundamental research. You have to look at the market and discover what your golf course can command. Failing to analyze your pricing structure is business suicide. Ascertain how much other courses with similar facilities are charging their golfers in "your" market. Know what the golf market is willing to pay. Then determine where your course fits into the picture based on your amenities, niche(s), and services and determine your rates based on your research and not your competitors. All these questions can be answered by doing an in-depth competitive overview before settling on a price point. Focus on the competitors within a thirty-mile radius of your course. This is as far as you'll ever pull the majority of your core customers from, so don't waste your money or time outside of this radius. You must determine whether your market will support your projected price point before publishing them and setting them in stone.

As I was conducting my initial research, I also needed to discover a universal price point for my product (the introductory membership), which meant I had to go far beyond the local market and look at prices from a national viewpoint. I had to analyze the pricing of almost twenty thousand golf courses across the United States, uncover a national average, and divide the average golfer's usage by that price to determine the average price of an eighteen-hole round. Then I multiplied that number by the number of visits recorded by casual golfers to introduce a realistic number that could be used as a hook to grab the attention of the untapped market. Once I had that number, I had to test numerous number combinations to determine which numbers were going to have the biggest draw. This formula didn't come to me overnight. It took a while, but it was worth the time, money, and effort. You need to create your own formula when settling on your pricing structure.

I was very fortunate because I had a good idea from the campaigns I had launched for health clubs, and there were similarities because some of the high-end athletic clubs had membership rates comparable to those in numerous golf courses, so at least I wasn't starting from scratch. I also had the benefit of the initial and ongoing consumer research I had from the health-club industry, which was applicable to the golf industry. One of the most difficult realities is getting people in the golf business to understand that MMC® targets consumers, not golfers. When you spend your time focused on golfers, you will soon run out of prospects and never grow the game or your business. When you focus on consumers with an interest in golf, your audience as well as your earning potential triples. Price offerings are hooks, and that is all they are. The most important component of a successful campaign is profiling your ideal customer and turning him or her into a golfer. I use price point solely as a tool to get my ideal customer in the door, not to give golf away.

Consumers with disposable income are highly intelligent, which is why they have disposable income. This is why I had to know the average number across the country and then within the thirty-mile radius of each of my clients' properties. Today's consumers are far more educated than those of past generations because all they have to do is go online, and within a couple of minutes, they know the very best deals available. They too, like your core golfers, know how to use a calculator and know about how many times they will golf in a year. If your customers are doing the research, don't you think you should too?

In chapter 2, I taught you how to professionally lock up relationships with golfers. In chapter 3, I taught you how to generate leads and market your course with little to no budget—i.e., grassroots marketing. And now in chapter 4, I have taught you how to use data and research to secure your market share. In chapter 5, I am going to show you how I took all the information in chapters 2, 3, and 4 and engineered MMC®'s Cash campaign, targeting the casual and nongolfer segments, which is revolutionizing the golf industry.

CHAPTER 5

REVOLUTIONIZING THE GOLF INDUSTRY

After profiling and then conducting in-depth studies of the casual and nongolfer segments' buying habits, my team found that 90 percent of the interviewees said cost, customer service, and convenience were their deciding factors when choosing a golf course, whereas only 10 percent attributed their decisions to course condition, amenities, and facilities. This is the polar opposite of the core and avid golfers, of whom 90 percent said course conditions, amenities, and facilities contributed to their buying decision. Part of the story told by our studies is that 90 percent of the customers surveyed who fell in the uncommitted category said they would be more likely to join if prices were lower, customer service was better, and the location was more convenient. I listened to the public and designed MMC®'s Cash campaign around consumers' unmet needs, wants, wishes, and desires, all the while making sure we did not discount the membership or devalue the product.

All this data proved I was on the right track. My entire career thus far was built on the theory that if I could just lower the barrier-to-entry, focus on volume, focus external marketing on the uncommitted segments, and focus internal marketing on promoting the profit centers, I could increase sales (revenue) tenfold. The key to a successful campaign is to do the complete opposite of what all the industry's "experts" preach. The industry "experts" brainwash owners into thinking they can charge exorbitant fees, including initiation fees or enrollment fees, and then forget about the golfers, who were locked into one- or two-year agreements. I saw numerous flaws in this model over the years, including the obvious: that it alienated a huge portion of the market and led to poor renewal (retention) rates. Only the hardcore golfer and/or the families pursuing the county-club lifestyle stayed committed to the club. Which of course worked well up until about 2003.

I am not saying you can't sell golf memberships for a premium, get rack rates for your green fees, or charge enrollment fees because you absolutely can. I am saying have a menu that promotes loyalty and long-term commitments while protecting the most desired (and therefore sellable) tee-times, while balancing out the membership base with casual and nongolfers who will gladly play during slow times and slow seasons. The reason this model hasn't worked in the past is because no one knew how to profile, engage, and lock up relationships with these two segments. Some golf courses think it is simply the price and cannibalize their market because they sell introductory memberships to core and avid golfers who complain and finagle until they are golfing during prime times but are paying introductory pricing. It's not the price that grows the game and business; it's penetrating new segments of the market.

Everyone in the industry is thinking short term. There are numerous studies done on how much it costs to acquire a new customer (golfer) as opposed to retaining an existing one. The average cost to acquiring a new golfer works out to be approximately six times more than it cost to retain an existing golfer. In short, you save six times the revenue by servicing and then renewing your golfers than by replacing your golfers. This is far from a revelation for most savvy businesspeople, although it may be for others, but even those who know this fact fail to understand it in relative terms. This number must then be added to the lifetime value of the golfer, not just the up-front revenue or the one-year membership contractual number, to realize the true value of the golfer.

Once you know the value of your golfer, you will know how much you can afford to spend to acquire a new golfer as well as how much you'll earn per golfer. There are some golf-course owners who are reluctant to try MMC®'s Cash campaign because they look at the hook (price point) only as a one and done without any additional fees; they are simply unaware of the true value of each golfer and the massive back-end revenue contributed by these elusive golfers. Owners know they need new memberships to continue the operation of the course, but they don't realize the impact a single new golfer has on the bottom line for years to come. This is why I am against programs such as discounted daily deals, because if the golfer is not engaged properly by the course staff, these programs are the classic one-and-done deals and will not grow the game or the business. It would be different if a staff member accompanied the golfer through the round, selling him or her on the membership like in the health-club business, but golf is a different animal. Most of the time, the golfers and guests check in at the pro shop, are thrown a key to a cart, and are never seen again. Until there is a professional sales system in place, discounted tee-times will never be a viable hook.

I want owners to start thinking about long-term revenue as opposed to what they need today. Each prospective golfer has a value; let's use X as that value and multiply it by how many golfers we can attract through a single marketing campaign. This is exactly what I did: the X amount (revenue raised) determined how much my clients could afford to spend on each campaign. I was focusing on the bottom line: how many new golfers the marketing campaign would attract, how much immediate and residual revenue the campaign was going to raise, and so on. Then I worked my way back through the numbers to determine how much money the course was going to invest (but of course, first I would raise the money) into MMC®'s Cash campaign to acquire each new golfer. After that, it was simple math to determine whether it was a good investment.

Another important aspect of knowing the real value of each prospective golfer is once you know the dollar value of each golfer, you tend to work harder on cultivating each relationship because you know the true value of the golfer is not just $30 (or whatever your green fees or membership dues are) but could end up being $5,000–$10,000 in future revenue.

I needed a way to lower the barrier-to-entry enough to attract the nonuser so that I could increase traffic and increase daily receivables through profit-center revenue, which in turn would offset or even surpass the revenue owners imagined they would lose. In short, I wanted to redistribute the revenue stream. I first thought of this from an experience I had when I was fifteen (1978). I was staying with my aunt and uncle in Chicago for a couple of months; they lived on Southport and Irving Park on the North Side, just a few blocks from Wrigley Field. One night, my cousins informed me we would be driving out to the suburbs the following day. Everyone was excited because we were going to a store called Walmart; I didn't share their enthusiasm because I had a summer job and worked all week in a warehouse, and the weekend was supposed to be for fun, not for driving a couple of hours through city traffic, crammed in the back seat of a tiny Ford Falcon, just to go shopping, when we had at least four grocery stores within ten blocks of their house.

Once we arrived at Walmart, I immediately understood why everyone was so excited. First, the parking lot was packed. Cars were everywhere, and everyone I saw was smiling and happy. You could literally see how excited everyone was to be there. People were scurrying through the parking lot to get through the store entrance; some were dressed to the hilt, some not so well, but most were just everyday hardworking people like my aunt and uncle. As we entered through the doors, everything was bright and beautiful. There were more products than I had ever seen in a single store. Kids were staring at toys with their mouths open wide in disbelief. Teenage boys and girls were playing with balls, bicycles, and electronics. Moms were looking through household products and clothing; dads were in the lawn-and-garden section. There was literally something for everyone. We all had a fantastic time shopping at Walmart that day, and the entire family went home with something.

I believe that was on a Saturday because the following day my uncle and I were sitting out on the front porch, people-watching and talking. I told him how cool Walmart was and how much I really enjoyed going there, and I thanked him for taking me. But even back then, I was very inquisitive. I was one of those precocious kids you call a pain in the behind when they are growing up but then are viewed as geniuses in their fields when they're older and successful. Like most kids, I had Teflon skin and didn't care whether people thought I was a pain in the behind or not; I was just being inquisitive. I asked my uncle why he drove all the way out there to shop when we lived in the middle of countless stores. His answer was really simple: "Because at Walmart, I can afford to buy a little something for everyone, and it's all under one roof." Now that was genius!

From then on, I studied models like Walmart and Sam's club, as well as their founder, Sam Walton. His philosophy was to serve the everyday consumer—the masses—and make his companies' money on volume and variety. I once read if you want to earn more money, give more value; if you want to earn even more money, give even more value to more people. Sam Walton knew this and implemented it on a mass scale. He knew the elite class was very small (less than 20 percent of the population), disloyal, and extremely difficult to penetrate, whereas the everyday consumer, comprising 80 percent of the population, was not only penetrable but also far more loyal. This is a very simple concept, yet some industry guys can't grasp it and still focus on the membership cost or green fee and not the enormous overall residual income that can be earned from thousands of happy, loyal new golfers.

I knew the first challenge was to find the magic number for the introductory membership, which would be so good no one could pass it up—basically, I wanted to make everyone an offer he or she couldn't refuse—but at the same time, it needed to be a number that could be universally successful in any geographical area. There have been numerous studies on number combinations and how they are received and processed by consumers. Do I use a four-digit number, a three-digit number, or a two-digit number? Should it end with an eight, a nine, a zero, and so on? These studies helped a lot with the academics of the campaign and provided the pertinent data, but the only way I would ever really know the answers to all my questions as well as the validity of my theories was by testing several combinations in the real world, and my answer would lie in the results.

There is a marketing reality called the pique technique. The pique technique teaches you to stay away from the norm when advertising. Human brains are lazy and take millions of shortcuts when processing things we see in an attempt to conserve energy. If our eyes see something familiar, our brains tend to scan over it and compartmentalize it because they assume they already know what is coming next. If you want your advertising to get noticed, the worst thing you can do is repeat the same offer over and over again (including repeating your competitor's offer). You have to change it up, or the consumer will soon be immune to it.

I knew ninety-nine dollars had worked extremely well as a hook a decade ago because that was the number we used in the health-club industry, but by the late 1980s and early 1990s, many health clubs were copying and abusing the ninety-nine-dollar hook, and consumers were seeing it everywhere. That is still one of the biggest problems that plague the golf industry today—copycats. Course owners, managers, and pros see their competitors run a promotion, and without any research or education, they try to copy it immediately. These clueless geniuses don't realize they know only what their competitors, or whoever has designed the campaigns, want them to know. These golf courses that copy the offer are getting the same information being blasted to the consumer, and they are taking the bait just like the consumer.

This is an actual e-mail I received from a golf course in Ohio just last year, which hammers in this point. I was following up with a course manager/pro who had called our office (per his owner's request) requesting information on MMC®'s Cash campaign. When he picked up the phone and realized it was me, he said, "I don't have time for this BS," and hung up. A few minutes later, I received this e-mail:

"Chuck,

Sorry to be so blunt about it! When he first asked me to reply to you, he said to try to learn what I can, learn how you do what you do. Basically puts me in the awkward position of "how much can you tell me about your company without paying anything." I've talked extensively to other companies before, with no intention of buying anything. He's never acted on anything as far as duplicating, but he has taken in a lot of free knowledge to put to use for himself, so I commend him for that, I guess! I'm reaching the time of year where I am getting too busy to play his head games, so I just wanted to be frank with you. Thanks and good luck!

Regards"

Think of launching a marketing campaign like MMC®'s Cash campaign as going fishing; before ever baiting a hook, you must have a detailed plan. The night before, as you prepare for the event, you decide on what species you want to fish for (demographic); which location you'll fish in (geographical area); what bait you'll fish with (offer); the habits of the species of fish you are targeting (lifestyles); the depth to which you'll fish (what days and times you want your marketing to hit the public for the fullest impact); whether you need to bring additional equipment, such as bobbers, different-sized hooks, lures, and so on (supplemental media); whether you're fishing all day or overnight (duration); and what the migration habits of the fish are (how you keep your current golfers in place and how to prevent them from migrating to the new offer), as well as a thousand other questions that must be answered before you even leave the house and most of the answers must be made based on years of experience and data. You just don't say, "OK, I have the hook and a worm. Now, let me go compete with the pro anglers." Yet people somehow hypnotize themselves and others into believing they know how to run their neighbors' campaigns.

I have come to understand this phenomenon of taking the path of least resistance well as I study the industry. I put people who choose to rely on their competitors for new ideas into two classifications—the too busy and the morally challenged. The too-busy person busts his or her butt all day, wearing more hats than a hat rack can hold. This person does every task in the business. Whether this onslaught has been self-imposed or assigned, it is a recipe for overload, mismanagement, and inevitable burnout. The morally challenged, on the other hand, are so afraid of losing their jobs or being failures that they spend more time in fear than on innovation. People like this are always looking for the shortcut—the easy way. I am not going to say there are no shortcuts in life, because there is at least one: it's called accelerated learning, and if you use it wisely, the knowledge you acquire can be used to catapult you far beyond your competitors. But you must know when a shortcut is a shortcut and not a path that leads you over a cliff.

The majority of golf-course owners normally get into the business because they are golf enthusiasts. They live, eat, and breathe the game, just as I live, eat, and breathe marketing and professional sales. They come into the industry for the right reasons: to provide a valuable service for an honest return. People go into business to serve others and make livings. Unfortunately, a lot of the morally challenged have made it extremely difficult to earn a good living in the golf business today. These morally challenged have skimmed the top off the business to the point that every golf course in America must work ten times harder just to get by. I have never seen times as difficult as they are today in this business, and it is absolutely avoidable, especially when you read the data on the percentage of Americans interested in golf. Later, in the final chapter, I will lay out a detailed plan to get the industry back to its glory days, but right now, I'm getting ahead of myself, so back to the membership that is revolutionizing the golf industry.

The ninety-nine-dollar offer was a huge draw, but like everything, when the newness wore off, the response dropped off as well. So I needed to make a new twist on an old hook. Always remember it's a waste of time to try to reinvent the wheel. Just complement the original design by making it better, faster, cooler, smoother, and so on, which is completely different from copying. The wheel is a wheel, but you can compare the wheel off a horse's buggy from the eighteen hundreds next to a one-off rim from a custom 2017 Escalade, and although both of them are wheels, there is a world of difference between them. A golf-course membership is a golf-course membership, and there is no reason to change the product, but the price point, packaging, and presentation of the membership are only hooks, and a hook needs to be changed.

I really liked the response from the ninety-nine-dollar hook, and since the amount collected at the point of sale played a major role in making the campaign successful and self-funding, it was a perfect place to start. You must collect enough money up-front to pay for the expenses of the campaign, and you must also be able to show the owner an immediate ROI, or he or she will never agree to move forward with the campaign. But as I said, I couldn't use ninety-nine dollars as the hook because everyone in the business was using it every day and killing its effectiveness. I could use it only as a frame of reference to design the new hook.

The challenge with any type of hook like this is selling course owners on the idea. Most owners are not marketers or salespeople. It is very difficult for them to think far enough outside the box to understand that the price is just a marketing hook to grab golfers' attention. Owners get their information from their pros, industry magazines, their competitors, or other owners and industry people. Unfortunately, sometimes when it comes to growing the game or a business, it is the blind leading the blind, especially when it comes to marketing and sales. When owners hear a hook like the ninety-nine dollars, they automatically think it's too cheap and that the price point will ruin their businesses, because again all they see is the price point and not the overall revenue. They assume the program is a fire sale designed to get a bunch of cash up-front and to hell with tomorrow. From the commencement of this new marketing strategy, I had to make sure MMC®'s Cash campaign was going to be engineered to bring in daily receivables, monthly receivables, member loyalty, and tons of up-front cash collected at the point of sale as well as long-term residual income for years to come.

Course owners tend to focus so intently on rack-rate membership or green fees that the Grim Reaper of being cash poor creeps up and bites them in the butt. Then, and only then, do they change their focus to raising cash, but unfortunately, it is out of desperation instead of forward thinking. They now lose focus of memberships and make desperate attempts to raise cash through discounted green fees. It has always been a challenge to balance up-front cash with long-term residual revenue. I was determined to rectify all that by creating a campaign that would not only bring in obscene amounts of cash but also increase daily revenue, as well as monthly receivables. And guess what—I did exactly that.

I had the number I was going to use, and no, it was not ninety-nine dollars. That was no longer the magic number. It had been beaten to death, and everyone knows there is no reason to flog a dead horse. Now I needed to design a membership that was attractive enough to get people to say yes but perfectly balanced between value and investment. My goal was to design an introductory membership with parameters built in to create a bottleneck effect that would funnel the new golfers into playing during the slow times and seasons in order to balance out the tee sheet, leaving the peak tee times for the existing members and core golfers who are willing to pay more.

As I discussed briefly in the previous chapters, I tested numerous ideas, such as off-peak hours, special events, summer memberships, two-for-ones, buy-one-get-one-free offers, and on and on, but none ever worked at the magnitude I needed. All these campaigns were successful on various levels, but I wasn't looking for mediocre results; I was looking to revolutionize the golf industry. I finally decided on limiting the days. I knew most golf enthusiasts tried to golf on weekends—for example, Saturday and Sunday—although most core and avid golfers did their best to tee off before 10:00 a.m. I also knew from experience that you could shoot a cannon through most golf courses on Monday through Thursday without hitting a single golfer (although that has changed a little in the past decade thanks to MMC®).

There were a few courses that offered a Monday-through-Friday golf membership for a fraction of the cost of a full membership, which on the surface sounds like a brilliant idea, except for the fact they sell those memberships to core and avid golfers, who would have paid the published rates. What most golf-industry people don't know is that model was borrowed from the health-club industry.

In the late 1980s, I designed a five-day membership for use during the slow days to offer as a hook to grab the attention of the deconditioned market. This five-day membership was only offered to this new segment (untapped market) and not to core health and fitness enthusiasts. But of course, the person who borrowed that hook and brought it to the golf industry wasn't privy to the design and, therefore, the strategy, so he or she offered it to core and avid golfers. Again, this was someone just skimming the surface for a quick fix.

I chose to stay with the proven formula and designed my first membership to be a five-day introductory membership specifically targeting the casual and nongolfer. This would bring in new golfers during the slow days while freeing up the weekends for the core membership and free up plenty of tee-times for green-fee play. Most operators worry so much about being too busy on the weekends and slow play that they forget about Monday through Friday.

A large portion of core and avid golfers want to play on weekends and more specifically want to tee off between 6:00 a.m. and 10:00 a.m. This is the reason why courses that incorporate this five-day membership on their own only are lucky if they acquire a couple of hundred golfers as opposed to MMC® that acquires over twelve hundred golfers on average—MMC® targets casual and nongolfers while the courses who choose to do it on their own are limited to the core and avid golfer market(s).

When courses attempt to copy MMC®'s campaigns, they fail miserably because they have absolutely no way to target the casual and nongolfer, leaving them with only core and avid golfers. Some core and avid golfers will buy the limited-day membership and try to golf every day, which creates more problems than profit. Also, when the core and avid golfers are taken out of the market, the course has no future revenue. This concept can work only if it is specifically designed to acquire new business from a new segment(s) of the market that has never been tapped before. Selling this membership to core and avid golfers without balancing the scale with casual and nongolfers is financial suicide.

I tried numerous other offers in the beginning, but they failed to pull an acceptable response. I designed traditional campaigns like twilight and early-bird memberships that had modest returns. My challenge was that I was not hired for modest returns. When people hire me and MMC®, they want big results fast, and I was designing a campaign that could produce massive results immediately every time. I knew I would only have one shot at running each campaign because I was not an employee, and if I did not produce extraordinary results, I wouldn't be in the business long; there would be no mulligan for MMC®. I also knew my campaigns needed to produce consistent results as well. I needed a course in Ashville, North Carolina, to be able to generate the same revenue as a course in Chicago; Illinois; or Los Angeles, California.

When I was on the road meeting with course owners, I would have at least two or three owners a week tell me, "You may have raised two hundred thousand dollars in cash in such-and-such course, but you will never do that here. This town (or city, market, or state) is different; these people are different; our weather is different; our grass is different; our economy is different; and hell, our dogs are different." What most people don't understand is numbers are numbers, and business, as well as sales and marketing, is also based on numbers. The offers, amenities, price point, packaging methods, and so on need to be tailored to each individual course, but the buying habits and spending patterns of the casual and nongolfer segments are the same in every city, town, and state. As long as I had enough of a population that fit my profile within the courses' geographical reach, I knew I could get the same or at least similar results every time.

Almost all golf courses are basically the same on the surface—that is, private, public, muni, resorts, and so on—all sell nine, eighteen, twenty-seven, or thirty-six holes of golf. I designed a campaign to sell the experience and then factored in the differential advantages of my client's course. The golfing experience, course conditions, course design, course layout, pro shop, banquet rooms, restaurant and bar, and so on are the differential advantages that justify and encourage the up-sales, add-ons, and profit-center revenue. Every course has its own differential advantage over their competitors.

The differential advantages are the benefits a golf course has over its competitors. This may be a course's USP (unique selling proposition) or some advantage the course has through its operations, such as a beautiful clubhouse with banquet facilities, or the service it provides. It just takes a little time and research to determine your advantage over your competitors (and there could be numerous advantages) and highlight those selling points. As a golf marketer, I have to identify and highlight what advantages my clients have over their competitors and capitalize on those features, advantages, and benefits.

Marketing a golf course means discovering what advantages a golfer will receive by joining your loyalty program as opposed to your competitor's: find out what separates you from your competitors, what makes your course's rates better value than your competitors', and so on. Start learning by asking yourself good questions, and your brain will give you great answers. These are the same questions golfers are asking themselves: Which is better, golf course ABC or golf course XYZ? Why should I join ABC golf course over XYZ golf course? These questions are going through the golfers' minds, and you must have those answers readily available. Put those answers out in the front for your community to see.

One of the biggest hurdles I have to overcome to this day is how course owners immediately assume I am discounting the membership by selling it for a price point lower than their advertised rates. What they are failing to see is the overall concept of redirecting the revenue stream, volume and the lifetime value of each golfer. It is far better to have 1,500 golfers pay you $100 per year than to have one 150 golfers pay $1,500 per year (although the goal is to have both groups to be operating at peak performance), and here is why:

If you have 150 core golfers and they golf one hundred rounds each per season, as a group they are golfing fifteen thousand rounds. If they pay $1,500 per membership, you are collecting $225,000 for those fifteen thousand rounds, most of which will be consumed during prime times with very little profit-center revenue. On the other hand, MMC® brings you fifteen hundred casual and nongolfers who play ten rounds per year and as a group consume the same fifteen thousand rounds per season. This group pays $200 to join, which is $300,000 in up-front cash collected ($75,000 more cash collected at the point of sale), and then they spend on average $20 per round (most of which will be spent during off-peak times), bringing in an additional $300,000 their first year, which means you will collect $75,000 more at the point of sale plus an additional $300,000 per year in back-end revenue from your profit centers totaling $375,000 more in revenue in the very first year than you are getting from your core golfers. The course makes more money my way than it does the old way. The revenue is more than doubled (almost tripled) in just the first year when you add the cash collected and the first year's back-end revenue. Every year, the core members renew, and you receive $225,000 (less attrition), and every year the casual golfers are locked up, you earn another $300,000 in back-end revenue (less attrition) again $75,000 more per year than your core golfers.

With my model the average golf course is going to bring in $300,000 in cash collected at the point of sale and a minimum of two year's back-end revenue (because we lock the consumer/golfer into a two- or three-year relationship), bringing the projected revenue from just one of our campaigns to almost one million dollars in revenue in just ninety days. This estimate does not include revenue from other profit centers, for example, buddy-referral green fees, range revenue, outing revenue, banquets, leagues, lessons, clinics, merchandise, club storage, locker fees, trail fees, annual cart passes, social events, and so on. We only track the revenue derived from our clients' food and beverage sales and cart rentals for our studies, everything else is icing on the cake.

There are only a finite number of core and avid golfers within a geographical area willing to commit to a golf course by purchasing a membership, and even fewer are willing to pay $1,500 or more per year for a membership. You must also take into consideration all the other courses in the area that are competing for those same core and avid golfers as well. By grafting in these new segments a course increases their market by 200 percent. Remember, research proves course condition, amenities, and facilities are the most important to the core and avid golfers but far less important to the casual user. This means unless you are the top dog in your market, you must be creative with your marketing to make up for what you lack in prestige, amenities, facilities, course design, layout, length, condition, location, staff, and so on.

Another part of my team's research showed that golfers who spent $1,500 per year will spend significantly less day to day than the golfers who spent less than $100 per year. This segment (the casual users) will spend far more in your profit centers. The golfer who spends more expects more and doesn't expect to pay additional fees or spend more for other services, whereas those golfers who perceive they paid very little in comparison with value are more apt to spend even more than their counterparts because the spending is never perceived as a large amount of money. So, by having a larger portion of casual golfers, you will have a greater chance of increasing daily, monthly, and annual revenue.

This reality of casual users spending more in profit centers is completely foreign to most owners because they can only relate to what they know. Owners know that when they give discounts on tee-times the course attracts penny-pinching golfers who can squeeze eleven cents out of every dime. This is because the course is marketing the tee-times to core and avid golfers—not casual and nongolfers. My team sees this all the time. For example, on average, core and avid golfers as a group ride in a cart about 60–70 percent of the time, whereas the casual and non-golfers as a group ride in a cart about 90–95 percent of the time. MMC® profiles, engages, and locks up relationships with consumers who have disposable income—not penny-pinching core and avid golfers.

Deciding what to put in and what to leave out of the membership package is also crucial to the success or failure of each campaign not to mention the long-term financial health of the course. In almost every case, the owner, manager, and pro are completely off base when it comes to this part of the campaign. In the initial setup of every golf course's campaign, my team and I always consult with the course's owner and manager to get his or her input because no one knows the course's day-to-day business as they do. Unfortunately, in most cases, they are way too close to their own product to give unbiased input on what we should offer and at what price point; their opinions reflect their perceived value, not the reality of the marketplace. Because they have invested so much of their blood, sweat, and tears into the business and are always dealing with core and avid golfers, they look at the product with an unrealistic bias. It is too difficult for them to step outside of their cocoon and objectively view the course as the public does and even deeper—as the casual user does.

I designed the Cash campaign to help golf courses capture an elusive segment of the market. Courses were (and still are) struggling to capture their market share due to supply outpacing demand; for the record, this is the industry experts' opinion, not mine. I know the industry is not overbuilt; it is just inadequately marketed. There is still plenty of business for everyone if the powers that be will just get out of their own way and consider the possibilities of doing something other than what their neighbors are doing. Another obstacle for course owners to get over is to stop listening to the organizations and people who make their living off telling owners what they want to hear.

Albert Einstein defined insanity as doing the same thing over and over again while expecting a different result. Most people (yes, this includes golf-course owners) go through the cycle of insanity at least once in their business careers. The business runs great for a few years then things start to fall apart. One day they get to a point where the pain is so great that they have to change, so they take action. Soon the pain reduces, so they lose their drive or motivation. Then they stop taking action altogether and inevitably go right back to where they started. Most of the time, they are even worse off than they had been when they started. Now they have to take action again because the pain (motivation) has returned, which causes the vicious cycle of insanity to repeat.

You see this every day with people trying to lose weight. The pain is so great that they go on a diet, start to lose a little weight, start to feel better about themselves, and soon the pain is gone. Before they know it, they are hiding in a closet, eating a slice of cake with a bowl of ice cream. Within six months, they are heavier than ever and full of pain; time to start another diet—or, should I say, time to start the cycle of insanity again. Most golf courses are just doing the same old e-mail blasts, newspaper ads, and so on that they, their fathers, and their grand-fathers have done for the past five, ten, and even twenty years, or even worse, they are copying their competitors when they see something they think is new. Doing the same old advertising and promotions year after year is insane.

Students trained in popular marketing concepts insist the term for my marketing concept is *loss-leader marketing* (where something is sold at a loss to draw in customers). I strongly disagree and choose to call (and coined) this concept *lost-leader marketing* because my goal is to get course owners to identify with the concept of looking for resources they already have but have either overlooked or not discovered. *Loss* implies no longer having something, as when something is sold at a loss, whereas *lost* implies something is misplaced, forgotten, wasted or not taken advantage of, which can be found and used as a resource.

I find the areas of my clients' businesses that have been wasted and not taken advantage of as opposed to making them feel as though they must suffer a loss to draw in new golfers. It is not my intention to have them sell anything at a loss, nor do I want them to view this concept as having to lose something to gain something in return—a trade-off. MMC®'s Cash campaign is built around the concept of finding possible resources that may have been wasted or not taken advantage of—for example, slow times and slow seasons—and maximizing their potential. No client will lose anything; my clients only gain new golfers, hence the term *lost-leader marketing*.

Another one of my objectives for MMC®'s Cash campaign was to get existing golfers to remain loyal while other golfers gave the course a first or second look, which meant I needed to engineer a plan to keep exist-ing golfers from migrating over to the new introductory membership. I have seen the havoc fire-sale promotions have played on courses when a large portion of their core golfers switched over to a promotional offer. This will never happen with MMC®'s Cash campaign. I design each proj-ect with enough of a difference between my introductory membership and the course's current membership so that all golfers (existing golfers and new golfers alike) could clearly see the difference in value between the two memberships. I designed the program to generate repeat busi-ness (long-term revenue) as well as pull in unheard of amounts of cash at the point of sale. I was determined to make it a mathematical improbability (if not an impossibility) that all (or even a large portion) of the strong (repeat) relationships of the golf course would jump on our offer; my goal was to keep existing golfers in place with their existing memberships.

With my new introductory membership, I needed to assure course owners they were not giving the course away but using the introductory membership only as a hook to fill in slow times and drive revenue into the business during slow seasons, so I decided to use the airline industry as an example. Think of the seating arrangement in a passenger jet. The airline has a great deal invested in safety, equipment, personnel, training, fuel, licenses, computers, software programs, insurance policies, and so on. The airline's plane has an excellent first-class cabin with all the desired amenities; in addition, they have also developed a business-class cabin for the flyer who desires additional services but can't or won't pay for first-class accommodations. After the airline's first-class and business-class passengers get settled in, the owners look out over the seating of the airplane and realize over 85 percent of the seats are empty. Now, they still have to pay their pilots, mechanics, flight crew, safety inspectors, fuel costs, and countless other daily expenses, but they just can't sell enough tickets in the first-class and business-class cabins. Although the airline may have started off wanting to cater solely to first- and business-class passengers, they now see the need for another seating classification, so they decide to incorporate a coach class. Coach customers enter their cabin through the same door of the plane, they share the aisle and the air-conditioning with business and first class, and they arrive safely at their destination at the same time as first-class and business-class customers. But it is certainly not the same travel experience. Less than 5 percent of the plane is occupied by first-class passengers; now add an ambitious 10 percent for business class, which means the plane comprises 85 percent coach-class passengers and only 15 percent upper class. But keep in mind it is the coach-class customers who make the trip affordable for first- and business-class travelers as well as profitable for the owners and stockholders. If the entire plane were first-class seating, travelers would pay ten times the amount they pay today, and most airlines would be out of business—there are nowhere near enough travelers with that kind of disposable income to sustain several businesses catering to the same market.

several businesses catering to the same market.

My approach was to design three levels of golf membership, starting with an entry-level membership (with limited days of use) with a lower barrier-to-entry, and all other services (outside of a basic golf membership) à la carte. I repeat: this system is not discounting your green fees or membership dues; it is simply grafting in a new membership category and redirecting the revenue stream. You collect less up-front but far more over the term of the membership.

Next is a midlevel membership with no limitations on the days of use; the golfer pays more up-front and also follows the same à la carte system. In most cases, under this membership plan, these golfers pay as much or even more than the golf course is receiving from existing golfers under its current rate structure.

The final membership is the full all-inclusive membership you might currently have in place today. This is the membership level everyone will secretly aspire to. These are the golfers who golf once or twice a week, want to play during prime times and reserve the tee-times well in advance, want people to know their names when they come in the pro shop, want to play in all the course's events and leagues, don't want to be charged additional fees, want to walk in the clubhouse and get immediate attention and recognition, want to attend the social functions, and so on. This quality of service, attention, and unlimited access commands a premium membership fee.

To continue with the airline analogy, customers who have flown for many years hate the new airline à la carte business model. In the same way, your core and avid golfers will hate the new introductory offer and, therefore, will be unlikely to migrate to the new à la carte membership, feeling they will be nickeled-and-dimed to death. On the other hand, customers who are new to flying and not conditioned to the old flight package love the new à la carte model, perceiving it as paying only for what they use. This will be the same reaction from the casual and non-golfers and the millennial generation that is unfamiliar with the original membership model.

It is difficult to change the preconditioned buying habits of an existing golfer, whereas it is very easy (with the proper training of your staff and structuring of the offer) to condition the buying and spending habits of a new golfer. Unlike the airline industry, I believe existing preconditioned golfers should be allowed to keep their status quo, while most of the new golfers acquired from the casual and nongolfer segment are brought in on a new à la carte membership with the option of upgrading to an all-inclusive platinum membership. I knew from years of experience the only way this model would work was if my company (MMC®) tailored the memberships around the courses' existing business model. There was no way I was going to be able to design a cookie-cutter campaign or a one-size-fits-all type of campaign. Each project would be unique to each golf course.

The greatest challenge to this model of acquiring new golfers with a limited membership was the lack of core and avid golfers and the damn-near impossible task of reconditioning existing golfers' habits, both spending and lifestyle. I knew from past trials that core golfers wanted to golf Friday, Saturday, and Sunday and, most notably, between 6:00 and 11:00 in the mornings. I needed to work around the busy times and bring in golfers when the course was dead. I would need to design my campaign to target the untapped market that no golf course had the resources to identify, engage, or lock up relationships with and then condition those new golfers to use the course during slow times and slow seasons. Our campaigns also had to be designed with parameters built into the introductory offer, creating a bottleneck funneling the new consumers/golfers into playing during slow times and slow seasons, balancing out the tee-sheet.

With this approach to marketing, MMC® could successfully convert fickle price-jumping golfers into committed, loyal, free-spending members of their new golfing homes. At the same time, I would capture two new segments and get them locked up in long-term relationships, which would balance out the model. Core and avid golfers golf anywhere between 25 and 150 rounds per year, whereas casual or nongolfers will golf an average of ten rounds per year (as a group). So for every one hundred fifty core or avid golfers, each course needs to have twelve to fifteen hundred casual and nongolfers to balance out the model. Both segments will play the same amount of rounds; that is, the core and avid group of one hundred fifty golfers will average fifteen thousand rounds per year, and the casual and nongolfer group of one thousand five hundred golfers will golf fifteen thousand rounds. The revenue will be balanced as well. The core and avid golfer will be paying a premium rate for their membership but will rarely spend in the profit centers unless the course has a food or club minimum. On the other end of the scale, the casual and nongolfers will be paying a lesser fee for the membership but will be spending like "good-time Charlies" in the profit centers. These segments (casual and nongolfers) are not addicted to the game but are there for the experience, whereas core and avid golfers are saving every nickel so that they can get their fix by playing one more round.

Once a course has a golfer in a committed relationship, the staff have the time to solidify the relationship and sell the new golfer on staying loyal. You can do the same when selling your products or services. The same process I used to design my Cash campaign can be applied for any golf product or service: do your research, know your target market, and adjust the pricing and model accordingly. Remember, the hardest thing about the golf business is getting golfers through the door. Once he or she is on the property, you need to focus your attention on locking up the relationship. After that, it's all about customer service and retention.

Everything in life is perception (because people's perceptions are their realities). Golfers must perceive the value of the savings they are receiving as an enormous deal; at the same time, you must make sure you are not tarnishing your brand in the marketplace. This is a delicate balancing act, but it can be accomplished with properly designed marketing campaigns and experience. Look at your marketing programs and review what you have to offer: your profit centers, your memberships, and all the different possible revenue resources available. You want to make sure your prospects and community are going to associate nothing but good feelings and positive emotions with your golf course. Start thinking of some buzzwords, keywords, or phrases you know are going to resonate with your golfers. Think of your market, and think of some of the characteristics you would love to know about a golf course if you were in the prospect's shoes. Think of things that would attract you.

Think of words that describe emotions that would trigger positive feelings and incorporate them into your marketing and advertising.

Golf-course marketing requires thinking about the value of your brand in terms of its emotional equity: How does it make your prospects and golfers feel? Once you know how they feel about being golfers and golfing at your course, capitalize on those positive emotions and convey them in your ad copy and ad design. There are two questions you must ask yourself before launching a campaign and then stick the answers into your ad copy. First, "Can I justify customers buying my products and services now?" Second, "Can I prove to them why they need to buy it now?"

One of the early things I learned when studying marketing was the acronym FAB. FAB stands for features, advantages, and benefits. It is extremely important to highlight a product's or service's advantages over its competing products and services and the benefits derived by the prospect choosing those products or services over their competitors'. Since learning this acronym, I have made it a point to outline the features, advantages, and benefits of all my clients' courses because these FABs (fabulous selling points) will make prospects choose my clients' courses over their competitors' most of the time.

Success doesn't happen by accident; it happens by design. Unless you own an ultraexclusive golf course with a waiting list, you should think of your business as a numbers game—the more the golfers, the more the revenue. All that should matter when it comes to golf-course marketing (other than that it is done with dignity and integrity) is the ROI. The only way I know to sell anything is through ethical principles with the focus on the ROI.

Marketing and sales go hand in hand, and this is why I never understand how a golf course can hire a marketing company to launch a marketing campaign if the owner of the marketing company doesn't have a sales background. Marketing is sales to the masses; if you can't sell or don't know how to sell golf memberships to individuals, how on earth can you sell to the masses? Even worse, the marketing company cannot train the course's staff on the fundamentals of the campaign to sell the advertised product. To me, this is a huge disconnect. Keep in mind, the people who develop the marketing campaign should have the advantage of knowing how to present that product or service to ensure the integrity of the brand. The company hired to launch the promotion must train the existing staff on how to present the promotional offer.

As an owner, you can never let a promotion company bring in an outside sales staff to present your golf course. Building the relationship between the new golfer and the course is the key to building member loyalty. If an unknown salesperson sells the membership and then your staff have to reengage the new golfer and try to build another relationship, it can make the new golfer feel as though he or she is being shuffled around. This reflects poorly on the course because the new golfer feels as though there is no stability or security within the business. It is even worse if the new golfer really connects with the salesperson and then discovers he or she is not going to be around in a month or so; the golfer will feel like a number as opposed to a valued golfer.

Throughout my years of traveling the country visiting courses, I have seen and heard the most outlandish sales presentations and representations of numerous courses' memberships by outside sales staff. After the promotion company is gone, the owner and staff are left to clean up. I've had owners tell me the salespeople told prospects that the course will give free carts, golfers could bring in a guest with no additional fees, or the membership could be frozen or transferred, when the salesperson clearly knew the membership was nontransferable and could not be frozen, and, of course, the guest had to pay cart and green fees. These fly-by-night hucksters will say anything to sell the memberships and get their commissions because they know they will be down the road next month and couldn't care less about the carnage they leave behind.

Letting an outside sales staff come into your pro shop and sell to your golfers is like letting someone else tee off for you and then you playing the rest of the hole. If you're ever going to learn the game, you must be able to hit your driver, and if you're ever going to run a golf course, you must learn sales. As part of my program, I incorporate a professional sales system that anyone can follow, no matter his or her level of experience or skill set. In chapter 2, I went through an in-depth sales system for locking up relationships, but it takes years to master that system, and each of my campaigns are only forty-five to ninety days long at the very most. The duration of the campaign has to be short and sweet;

otherwise, you risk conditioning the market into thinking your membership is only worth X.

This is another reason you can incorporate a campaign like this into your marketing strategy only if you partner with an outside company like MMC® so you can explain to your core and avid golfers as well as the community that your rates have not changed; this is a one-time introductory offer designed by MMC® specifically to introduce nongolfers to the game.

I don't have five years to teach a course's staff my entire system; besides, most people wouldn't learn it even if I laid it out step by step, as I have done in this book. The fact is someone must love sales and marketing to give it the time it requires. I had to create a condensed version along with incorporating the key points of the sale into my marketing materials so that selling would now become order taking. Most courses are plagued with staff issues, so my campaign's sales system had to be designed so any staff member in the course could take the order. The system had to be engineered in a way that there was no need for sales skills. I wanted to be able to assure my clients there would be no need for additional staff because anyone from a student at the front desk to the bookkeeper in the back office could take the order with ease.

The only way I knew I could accomplish this was to ensure our marketing pieces and direct-mail pieces completely outlined the membership from content to cost. I knew there could be no miscommunication or confusion. I also wanted to involve the entire staff, from the front-counter person to the secretary in the back office, in the training, so that they would know exactly what we were offering and how to take the order, so that at no time would a golfer be left waiting, and every staff member would feel involved as an important part of the team. Involving the entire staff brings the team together for a common goal. I have always believed everyone in the business should be actively selling or at least prospecting for the course. Employees must know their paychecks are dependent on the course's ability to bring in revenue, and it is everyone's responsibility to make sure the course is growing. At the same time, I believe everyone should be compensated for their effort— for example, commissions, bonuses, or perks. Now that I had designed the introductory membership in a way that the membership could be written up by any staff member, it was time to perfect my delivery system.

Since I knew direct mail was going to give me the biggest bang for the buck and that I would be working with golf courses all over the United States, I thought the best place to start my research on direct mail was with mailing houses that have a national reach. You can find good printers just about anywhere in any town, but great mailing houses are a different story. It was extremely important to find a mailing house with existing long-term relationships with post offices and postmasters across the entire country. One of the things I quickly learned was that the day your mail hits your golfer's mailbox plays a major role in the response you get from your direct mail. Since there are a number of vendors with their hands on the direct mail, any one of them including the shipping company can kill your land date if they screw anything up. Other things like exterior presentation determine whether your piece ever sees the light of day or not, and on and on. Mailing houses can kill your mail if they make one little mistake in the mail-prep process or the handling, which can also get the pieces rejected by any one of the many post offices it must pass through before it goes into the carrier's bag for delivery. I also learned that if the mail is packaged, handled, prepped, loaded, shipped, and so on correctly, it can save you a ton of money and time. Direct mail is kind of like MMC®'s campaigns—knowing what not to do can be as equally important as knowing what to do.

I knew I had designed several great marketing pieces. I had been designing and testing numerous pieces over the years and discovered some invaluable nuggets to get huge responses, so I was determined to make sure some mailing house wasn't going to drop the ball and cost me a percentage of my response by making novice mistakes. My clients trusted me with their capital (even though the campaign raised the revenue first; it was still their capital), and I was not about to take unnecessary chances with that trust. I knew direct mail was the key to the success of the campaign as well as the key to the long-term success of the course's financial health, so I made it a priority to be well informed.

I needed to work with a company with years of experience; a company with the capacity to handle any volume; a company that stayed up to date on postal regulations and requirements; a company that had in-house postal verification; a company that had the respect of not only the post office but also other delivery companies such as UPS; a company that was centrally located in the United States so that mail drops and deliveries would be easier to calculate; a company that knew how to prepare the mail so that it got in mailboxes faster; a company that understood the ins and outs of the postal service in order to save on postage and time through drop shipping to USPS-SCF facilities; a company that could assure quick turnaround times; a company that could provide full-service printing, mailing services, fulfillment, and logistics, and these were just my basic requirements. I knew I had to partner with the best of the best, and I definitely knew I didn't have the time, the knowledge, or the staff to do what they did—especially after all my research. I am smart enough to know what I don't know.

At this point, I was well on my way to perfecting the campaign that would eventually revolutionize the golf-course industry. Through tireless research, practical experience, and a little common sense, I was able to develop a sophisticated demographic profile to identify my target (the untapped market), design marketing pieces that eliminated the need for professional salespeople, make the campaign self-funding so that there would be no upfront fees or out-of-pocket expense for the owner, create an offer and price point that would bring golfers in by the hundreds (if not thousands), build a team who was qualified to do 99 percent of the work behind the scenes so that the course's staff and ownership could focus on collecting the revenue and cultivating the new relationships, partner with the country's very best mailing house and list brokers, enlist the absolute best delivery system, and create a step-by-step action plan to manage all the working parts to ensure a successful campaign. There was only one thing left: How was MMC® going to get paid?

If you spend time around me, you'll hear me say, "This is one of the reasons I have been successful," and if you are around me long enough, you'll hear me say it hundreds of times, referencing hundreds of different things. With that preface, here I go again.

I feel one of the reasons I am so successful is I always put the other person first. I learned a long time ago that in any negotiation if you first unearth what the other person really wants (I emphasize "really" because most people tell you one thing but mean another) and think of how you can give it to him or her, you should easily be able to find a way to get what you need as well. This is truly how it went with the design of MMC®'s compensation plan. I literally designed everything before I ever thought about how we were going to be paid. Had I done it the other way around—thought of how much money we were going to charge first—I would have been putting the cart ahead of the horse. Look at it this way: How could I know the least I could accept until I knew exactly what it was going to cost me to produce and market the product?

Before you go into a negotiation, you must know what you can't live without and the very least you are willing to accept. So I sharpened my pencil and started going through the figures.

Since I had already done my research and locked up pricing with all the vendors, such as the list company and mailing house, I knew almost to a penny what my expenses would be. I was determined not to pass expenses on to my clients for things such as market analyses, consumer profiling, and competitive overviews because most owners would not have a frame of reference as to their importance relative to the success of the overall campaign and would, therefore, want to contest their necessity. There was no way I could get into this conversation every time I partnered with a new client to grow his or her business because I knew two of the keys to the campaign's success were data and research. So I had no choice but to factor these costs into MMC®'s hard costs like personnel, office overhead, and so on.

Just as I had to unearth the right price point for MMC®'s Cash campaign, I also had to determine a fair commission (or success fee) for MMC®. I was determined to find a number where the owner came out way on top, and I (the marketer) was treated fairly relative to my contribution and the value I brought to the business. Ironically, after running the numbers, the number I settled on was 20 percent (80/20) of the total cash brought in from MMC®'s Cash campaign. We would receive no back-end revenue—revenue from profit centers or renewals—unless the course owner asked MMC® to run a renewal campaign. The course's annual back-end revenue would normally mirror the cash collected at the point of sale. For example, if the course raised $100,000 in cash, then the back-end revenue was projected to be $100,000 per year for the duration of the campaign. If the membership was for two years and the course brought in $100,000 in cash, the campaign was projected to generate another $100,000 each year from the new golfers, which meant the campaign would generate an additional $200,000 in back-end revenue over the next two years, bringing the total revenue raised by MMC®'s Cash campaign to $300,000. But MMC® would be compensated only on the initial $100,000. In short, although MMC® was directly responsible for $300,000 in revenue, we are only paid on the $100,000 collected at the point of sale, making the real percentage paid to MMC® more like 4 percent of the total revenue generated for the business. I felt this was a number no one could argue with.

Over the past twenty-five years, prices for everything have increased, but MMC® has never increased our commission. In 1991, it was 20 percent, and today in 2017, it is still 20 percent. I am proud to say the same for MMC®'s vendors. Twenty-six years ago, we agreed on pricing, and although paper, wages, insurance policies, rents, and most all other business expenses have increased, our vendors have never raised their prices because they were able to offset some costs thanks to new technology. The only prices that have increased with MMC®'s Cash campaign are those we have no control over: postage, local newspaper ads, radio advertisements, and so on. This is why building the right relationships with credible, competent people and companies are paramount to ensure the longevity of any business.

With MMC®'s success fee in place, I was now confident I would have no problem selling this "lost-leader" marketing concept of offering an introductory membership with a lower barrier-to-entry to untapped segments of the market because it was truly owner friendly and absolutely the best marketing campaign the golf industry had ever seen. I took all the risk out (risk reversal) by making the campaign completely self-funding and self-propelling. I eliminated any suspicion of fraud or misrepresentation because no one in my company (including myself) ever collects one dime of the membership money being paid by the new golfer; the course's staff would collect all the money and deposit it into the owner's bank account, not ours. The course pays the vendors directly from the funds raised through the Cash campaign. The course pays MMC® its success fee every Monday from the previous week's revenue, so that at no time would there be a question as to whether MMC® deserves a payment or not; the proof is in the numbers. My Cash campaign includes tons of upgrades and add-ons for future growth, ensuring the financial health of the business long term. The campaign was absolutely a no-brainer—or was it?

CHAPTER 6

BREAKING DOWN WALLS AND SHATTERING ANTIQUATED IDEAS

I had just spent the better part of five years constructing the greatest campaign that had ever been seen by the golf industry. Nowhere on earth could you find a legitimate, honest, legal, ethical way of making such a massive ROI than you could with my Cash campaign. Everyone won: the club owner won because he acquired new golfers with absolutely no risk, no upfront fees, and no money out of pocket, the campaigns raised hundreds of thousands of dollars at the point of sale, and the traffic brought in a ton of revenue for the following two to three years. Member loyalty was guaranteed because these new golfers were in a committed long-term relationship they loved. Golfers won because they got to be a part of the area's best golf courses for a fraction of the published rates. The employees won because their course stayed in business, providing them with long-term employment. I had no doubt in my mind that once the word got out every golf course in America would be knocking on my door.

I had spent most of my adult years traveling, so I wasn't worried in the least about hitting the road to visit golf courses. I had also sold over 500 health clubs on the promotion I designed for that industry, and the Cash campaign I had engineered for the golf industry was far superior to anything an owner had ever seen before. It was around October 2005 when I was ready to launch MMC®'s golf division. It took five years, even though I had the foundation from my previous research, because I had never worked for a golf course and needed to learn the golf industry.

I needed to know how industry people spoke and thought, just as I needed to study the casual and nongolfer to engage them as potential members. I needed to study course owners, managers, and pros. I knew most seasons in the Northeast and Midwest started in April and ended after Labor Day, so I decided to launch the new division in October so that I would be engaging owners during their off-season.

I mailed out a postcard to almost twenty thousand golf facilities, and I just knew I was going to have a hundred calls. The postcard was very similar to the one I had sent to health-club owners over the years, and they had always pulled extremely well. The first week went by, and not one call; the second week, not one call; and then the third. I was dumbfounded. I knew the industry was on a decline, and I couldn't figure out what was going on. I had done extensive research and spent hundreds of thousands of dollars during the process, and I knew I was doing everything right. I went over every detail with a fine-tooth comb and couldn't find one mistake. After about a month, I got a call from a golf course in southern Illinois. On the other end of the line was the owner of the course, who also happened to be a PGA member. Typical scenario: he was a pro who always wanted to own his own golf course and one day was able to scrape enough money together and put a down payment on a twenty-seven-hole facility in the middle of a subdivision. He was calling me from the clubhouse, sitting at his desk with a space heater on because the course was buried in snow, and it was cold as an iceberg outside.

He said he had received the postcard about a month ago and didn't believe a word on it. I, of course, wanted to dig deeper, so I asked him several questions and discovered that in all his years in the business neither he nor other pros had thought in terms of dollars but more in terms of rounds. He also said he thought $250,000 in ninety days was horse crap, and it sounded like a scam or a get-rich-quick scheme. As I was listening to him, all I could think was, maybe that is part of the reason why the industry is struggling to recover, because no one thinks in terms of dollars. He continued to tell me how he gets sales calls all the time making outrageous claims, but when they are given the chance to prove themselves, they fall flat on their faces. He said he was only calling me to hear what line of BS I was selling since there was two feet of snow on his course and he was stuck in the clubhouse anyway.

After he spoke for a while and I had gathered some important background data, I went into my presentation. I knew one of the hurdles in my presentation was going to be that I had been in the health-club industry, because during my research I was informed that industry-golf guys stick their noses up at health-club industry guys and consider the health-club industry to be beneath them. I found this comical because many of the things I saw in the golf industry while conducting research came straight from the health-club industry. For example, I started doing five-day memberships for our slow days in the mid to late 1980s, and as I wrote in chapter 5, I noticed many courses had just recently incorporated the same five-day membership for their slow days. Many health clubs allow members to keep their same rate year after year if they renew before a certain date using the "If you let your membership expire, you'll have to rejoin at the current rate" close, which has been a staple in the health-club business since before I was even in it. Punch cards came straight from the health-club industry as well as numerous other sales promotions and techniques. The health-club industry does have its black sheep, but the industry as a whole can teach every industry a thing or two about professional sales and marketing. The health-club industry is, was, and will always be based on sales, so why not learn from an industry that has perfected the art of growing a business?

After a long conversation, the owner started warming up to the idea. His concerns and objections were exactly what I had anticipated. One of the first questions I always get is "Can I really bring in that much cash and that many golfers within only ninety days, in the off-season, all at no cost to me?" Since the turn of the century, golf-course owners have been used to struggling and considering themselves extremely lucky if they have two hundred loyal golfers; they can't even imagine a thousand golfers. This is because they are brainwashed by industry numbers that tell them there are only so many golfers in a given market and that they can host only X number of rounds. These geniuses should qualify that understatement by saying that there are only X core golfers, X avid golfers, X casual golfers, and X nongolfers, and based on the segment (as a group), they each play a different number of rounds each year. The industry experts have tunnel vision, focusing on avid and core golfers, and that tunnel vision is costing owners the business they love. I explained to the Illinois course owner how we would be targeting new segments of golfers and how they would play an average of ten rounds per year but spend far more than most of his current golfers in his profit centers. So not only was I confident that MMC® could bring in $250,000 and more than a thousand golfers in the next ninety days, in the middle of winter, when the course was closed, but I was also just as confident that the course would see an increase in food-and-beverage sales, range revenue, merchandise sales, cart revenue, outings, and so on, which would increase its annual revenue for the next two years by at least $250,000 per year starting the following season as well.

After a couple of more conversations, he pulled the trigger, and we launched the campaign in January 2006. Within ninety days, we had brought in over $330,000 in cash, and not one golfer had hit a single ball. This guy sat in his office with his space heater the entire winter and just took one phone order after another. This first campaign that I launched for a golf course was a grand slam. The response rate was awesome; the upgrades from the five-day to the seven-day membership hit almost 30 percent, and migration of existing members to the introductory membership was negligible. I had done it. I had the perfect membership package, price, and delivery system. The course owner had more cash than he had ever dreamed of; there were over a thousand new golfers (with the majority coming from an untapped market), which drove up daily revenue in the profit centers by 200 percent from the new traffic on the slower days of the week. The campaign completely paid for itself; this course's name was now in the mind of every qualified resident in the immediate area, and these new golfers were bringing in friends and relatives paying the rack rates. Everything was perfect. The Monday-through-Friday membership targeting the casual and nongolfers was the perfect draw and balance of value relative to investment.

To say the least, he was ecstatic! This guy had been in the golf industry his entire adult life and had never seen anything like it. He was a believer and wanted to share it with the world. A year later, he came on board with MMC®. Soon after, he sold his course and has been representing our campaigns for over a decade. This was my first golf course, and the program went exactly as planned. I was lucky, though, because this guy was a go-getter, and he did everything exactly how I asked him to and never once gave me pushback. People tend to work a lot harder when it is their behinds on the line, and since he was the owner/operator, he gave it his all.

My Cash campaign was now a proven, performance-based, data-driven, worry-free, turnkey golfer-acquisition campaign, specifically designed to acquire new golfers from two new untapped segments through a no-risk self-funding marketing campaign. I had every objection in the world covered with a rebuttal that would make my campaign a no-brainer—or so I thought.

I soon realized that by naming my company Mulligan Marketing Concepts®, I actually had committed a faux pas because most pros consider a mulligan as being against the rules. What pros didn't realize was that this campaign was designed as a second shot at growing the game as well as the industry and a chance to relive the glory days of the 1990s. Pros might not take a mulligan, but 99 percent of all other golfers do. Besides, the way the golf business was going, most properties desperately needed a mulligan, which in my eyes is a do-over without a penalty or cost which by the way, describes MMC®'s Cash campaign perfectly. The golf industry was going through a downturn, and a mulligan was exactly what it needed!

Now that I had a course that had successfully completed the campaign under my belt, I knew I needed to get on the road. As I drove from state to state, town to town, and course to course, I received one polite dismissal after another. Golf courses have never seen a business climate like this. For a century, courses have been in control of their own futures and never really had to learn sales or how to market their products, much less penetrate new segments of consumers. The American dream was to get rich, retire, and play golf. Golf was a rung on the ladder of success, and courses just waited for the next generation to climb the ladder. They never expected this downturn and, therefore, never prepared for it. Marketing campaigns were frowned upon as discounting golf, and discounting was a four-letter word in the golf industry. Golf was way too precious and prestigious to discount. Most industry guys were in shock and felt the best thing to do was hunker down and wait out the storm.

I could see most of these guys were scared to death because this environment was completely foreign to them. Here is the reality of this industry: Owners look to their managers and pros to grow their business, and under ordinary circumstances, they are more than capable to do so when it comes to engaging core and avid golfers, but in this storm, they are ducks out of water. It's important to be perfectly clear that I am not diminishing the capabilities of a golf pro; what I want you to understand is that golf pros are trained in the game, public relations, and preparing budgets. People skills are taught by accreditation programs in a way to make the pro respectfully submissive to owners, members, and guests, which is great for customer service but not so great for growing the business, especially in this perfect storm. Accreditation programs teach pros how to dress appropriately and talk to members while, at the same time, the instructors are looking to weed out the drunks and the undesirables. They teach their golfers the game and etiquette. Yes, they are taught how to make a budget, but they are not taught how to sell or market the product to increase revenue. Most courses focus on public relations and the game while teaching very rudimentary business skills. "Why is that?" you ask. Because the industry always sold itself up until 2003.

There was no better way of learning what was really on owners' and pros' minds than being out on the road. Every course I visited provided me with new insights of what everyone was really thinking and feeling. I felt as though I had entered a cult because everyone I met was saying exactly the same thing as if they were reading from a teleprompter. It never failed to amuse me when I would be in a presentation and bring up the suggested price point for the introductory membership, and the pro, owner, or manager would gasp as though I had just dropped the F bomb and say, "Oh, we could never sell a membership for that. We never discount our memberships." Yet just twenty minutes ago, they had shared how they were offering cart and green fees for as low as ten dollars for eighteen holes with a third-party tee-time and green-fee vendor. When I did the math, they were discounting green fees by as much as 90 percent (after discount and split with the third party) and not getting anything in return, other than ten bucks or an online tee-time reservation system that could have been bought and kept in-house for a couple of bucks.

Earlier in the book, I explained the barter system and how courses can trade out rounds or other products and services for professional services. Most third-party tee-time vendors offer (prefer) barter options for using their online tee-sheet service and POS system, and for the exchange, they receive anywhere between one and ten rounds per day, including a cart (of course, their goal is to get as many rounds as they can negotiate in the trade-out). This barter, on the surface, sounds sensible because in many cases, the vendor is willing to accept off-peak tee times in the exchange, but even with off-peak tee times, the cost to the course owner can add up fast, and vendors discount the traded rounds extremely low so that they can sell their rounds first. The sad fact is the vendor actually competes for sales with his own client, choosing to sell his bartered tee times below market value to ensure the vendor gets his money first.

We worked with a golf course in California that had an agreement with a third-party tee-time vendor that was charging eight rounds a day. This company was discounting the fees so low that the vendor was killing the course. This vendor was advertising cart and green fees for ten dollars when the courses' rack rates were thirty-four to sixty dollars for the same times. Even if you split the difference, you could do the math with $22 as a base multiplied by the eight rounds, equaling $176 per day, $5,280 per month, and $63,360 per year. If they kept this up for over ten years, they would pay the third-party vendor almost $650,000. That wasn't even the worst part. This course was struggling to get anyone to pay their rack rates because the golfers had been conditioned to this third party's rates. Their constant advertising of cart and green fees for ten dollars was destroying the club financially and killing the brand. This course had no chance of increasing rates or the perceived value of the brand.

Many of these third-party tee-time vendors devalue the product beyond repair by selling and advertising green fees with cart for such ridiculous rates. They have made it nearly impossible for courses to get their rack rates because all their golfers reference the vendor rates and not the course rates. Their own golfers barely know the courses' names because all they know are the vendors' names and reference them as though they own the courses. These course owners are spending more time and money building the vendors' brands than they are building their own. I hope one of you honest people reading this book is in the business of building software so that you can give course owners a much better product for a fraction of the cost to host their online tee-sheet and throw in a POS (point-of-sales) system for free. Some of these companies are fleecing course owners, and, unfortunately, owners feel they have no choice.

All third-party tee-time vendors aren't so greedy though; some only charge one round of golf with a cart (for really high-end properties), but even with one round at $40 (still a deep-discounted rate), the third party is doing very well because $40 times thirty days is $1,200 per month and $14,400 per year, which comes to $144,000 over ten years, and for what? A simple platform to give golfers the opportunity to book online. This technology has been around for at least a decade. This software is so simple that a seventy-year-old with no interest, much less knowledge of technology, can operate it with ease. These companies try to confuse the owners by using terms like the cloud, online servers, and so on. They tell owners they must be on their server so that they can get updates and new features, 99 percent of which you don't need or want anyway. This is the biggest scam I have seen in decades, and the vendors are getting rich by selling courses space in a cloud just as a con man sells ocean-front property in Arizona (line from the George Straight song) all the while destroying most of their clients' businesses. I realize the technology of the cloud is far more sophisticated and complex than any layperson like me will ever know. My point is the end user's experience is dummy proof, and this technology is easily available for far less than what is being offered by most companies in the golf industry.

MMC®'s Cash campaign locks golfers up for two to three years so that you never have to devalue your product ever again. On the surface, it appears (by design) to be discounting because the ads must grab the attention of casual and nongolfers, but when you look deeper into the campaign, you will discover the golfer pays more on this type of membership and spends every golfing dollar in his or her new golfing home—your course. In addition, MMC®'s Cash campaign is only in the marketplace for ninety days and then is gone forever whereas these tee-time vendors are marketing their discounted tee-times every minute of every day for decades, conditioning the public to look for discounted tee-times, making discounting the norm and not a special offering.

Core golfers are the ones who really beat the system. They take a calculator to everything. For example, if they pay $1,200 a year for a membership, you can bet your bottom dollar they will do everything possible to play 120 rounds that year, so that they golf for $10 per round. The challenge with these golfers is that they will also do everything they can to avoid spending another dollar in the profit centers because most of them are on a fixed budget. If you take the dollar amount spent by the premium member (core golfer) and the introductory member (casual golfer acquired by MMC®) and average out how much is spent per visit, the introductory member will outspend the premium member over two to one as a group.

All those ten-dollar third-party golfers will now be paying rack rates to the owner and not to a vendor because you will no longer be discounting your rounds. Now you will have a balanced tee-sheet with casual and nongolfers golfing during slow times and core and avid golfers golfing during prime times. All the casual and nongolfers will be paying you (not a third-party vendor) twenty dollars on average per visit (during the slow times of the day) for the next two to three years, and they will play all ten of their rounds at their home course, and the best part is— you don't advertise the introductory membership for more than a few weeks, so the golfing community doesn't start to perceive the value of your course being less than your published rates.

Golfers no longer get conditioned to shopping for discounted rounds every day, because now golfers will only get the best prices direct from the course. Once the campaign is over, golfers will never see that price point again, and if they ask for it you can easily say, "That was a one-time offer we did with a company out of Florida, which specializes in growing the game, and our contract states once the campaign is over we can never offer that price point again. Besides that was their promotional introductory rate (similar to a corporate rate), not ours." Our membership and green fees are X and have never changed. If the golfer insists, you can say, "I'll be happy to extend the same rate to you as I did with MMC®, if you have a corporation with one thousand golfers ready to join and pay cash today."

Industry people must start looking at business (marketing) differently and realize they can either adapt or become farmers. There is no more "business as usual." The industry has changed, and no matter how much you hope, or wish, the Field of Dreams will come back, it's not going to. I often hear managers and pros say, "I hope we get all our events in this year, or I hope we host thirty thousand rounds this year, or I hope we get good weather this year." Well, I am here to tell you, hope is not a business plan nor is it a plan of action. The only thing that is going to work is—you going to work. I once heard, "Hard work always outperforms talent because talent doesn't always work hard."

One of the craziest things I was ever told by an owner was that he and "all" of his competitors had agreed not to lower their rates and stand firm with their current rates. I even heard this from two owners in the same market in Kentucky within a week. It is not unusual for two courses in the same market to call us at the same time when we send out solicitation postcards. We never disclose to either party the enquiry or the conversations. We never share any course's information because it would be unethical. We work with whichever course signs the contract first, but even then our prior conversations with their competitors are never discussed. These two owners called us, enquiring as to how we are able to bring in so many golfers. I went through the presentation with both of the owners and waited to hear back. About a week later, the owner of the stronger facility called me back and said he was very interested in moving forward but needed to hold off for a couple of months because of some personal issues that needed to be addressed immediately, but he was absolutely committed to move forward ASAP. A week later, the weaker course owner called me and informed me that although he was very interested in our campaign and needed the revenue badly he would be unable to run our campaign because he and "all" of his competitors had agreed not to lower their rates. I almost wet myself laughing (internally of course) at not only the absurdity of the statement but also that just last week his competitor made a commitment to run our campaign. This craziness is a recipe for bankruptcy. How can a weaker property strengthen its posture in a market if the owner agrees not to change his or her way of doing business? This was the best job of brainwashing I had ever heard of in my life. The big boys in town convinced some of the little guys to keep on doing what they were doing no matter what, which meant they could never grow their business and would eventually go under surrendering all the bankrupted course's golfers to the competitors just because of this one-sided agreement that was thought of by the two top courses in the area with the deepest pockets.

Over the past decade, I have heard of several courses that have gone out of business within just a couple of years of speaking with us, who failed to pull the trigger on our Cash campaign. They were so entrenched in their conviction of not "discounting" golf, they preferred to close the course rather than try something new. I remember this one course in North Carolina I had called on several times and followed up with every month for a couple of years, until one day I got a message saying, "This number is no longer in service." I couldn't believe my ears, so I had my staff do some digging, and they uncovered an article in a local newspaper, where the owner had cited there just weren't enough golfers to sustain the business and he was forced to close. I thought to myself, Bullcrap! I could have easily brought that course twelve hundred new golfers and it could have thrived, but instead of changing his prehistoric thinking, the owner preferred to close the course. His way, everyone lost—his golfers, his workers, his community, and most of all, his family. My way, everyone would have won, including the industry. Every time I see this (and I see it way too often) I think of a famous parable.

There was this old couple, and a drowning rain came, flooding the area where they lived. A warning came over the radio and television to evacuate immediately, but the couple refused to heed the warning. A few hours passed and the flood continued to rise when they heard a knock at their front door. Outside was a state trooper asking the elderly couple to accompany him back to the station for safety, but the couple refused, saying their "God would protect them." Several hours passed and the water rose even higher, and a rescue boat stopped in front of their home, the captain pleading with the elderly couple to get in the boat and let him take them to safety, but still the couple refused, saying their "God would protect them." The following day the couple was perched on their rooftop with the floodwaters engulfing their home. A helicopter was hovering above with a ladder lowered to rescue the couple and still they refused, repeating their "God would protect them." Sure enough, the couple got swallowed up by the floodwaters and perished. As they stood in front of their God, they asked, "Why did you not save us?" and their

God replied, "I sent you a state trooper, a boat, and a helicopter. What more could I do?"

Just as with any product or service, I realized there were core objections I needed to overcome in reference to my Cash campaign. The price point sounded too cheap to owners and pros (like discounting) even though my casual golfers outspend core golfers two to one. Course owners were also concerned about staffing issues, for example, whether their staff could sell the memberships and handle the calls and the increase in traffic, which of course is a nonissue since our marketing pieces outline the offer from cost to content, eliminating the need for salespeople or additional staff. Some owners felt MMC®'s success fee (commission) was too high because they only saw the 20 percent of the cash collected at the point of sale and neglected to see the enormous back-end revenue the campaign produced, bringing our real commission to about 4 percent of the revenue generated, and the cost of direct mail, which of course is paid with funds raised from the campaign. However, one of the major challenges wasn't an objection but had to be addressed often and that was getting owners to keep their hands off the initial cash raised so that it could fund the direct mail. Once the cash starts flowing, some owners lose their focus and start thinking of ways they can spend it, for example, taxes, bills, equipment. They quickly forget the initial cash has been raised specifically to fund direct mail in order to penetrate an untapped market.

Owners don't comprehend the importance of profiling consumers in different segments and fail to understand that different media target different demographic profiles. Eighty percent of MMC®'s marketing efforts are focused on targeting casual and nongolfers with only 20 percent of our marketing overlapping the core and avid golfer segments. Because marketing to core and avid golfers is cheaper and far easier, some owners want to divert 100 percent of the marketing dollars to the wrong media, which defeats the whole purpose of the campaign and destroys the business.

Course staffing issues are a concern I often run into not only because owners are fearful their staff cannot handle the sales or the influx of golfers but also because owners are concerned the new golfers won't be serviced properly. I always stress that I have removed the need for a sales staff altogether and that my campaigns require order-taking skills and not sales skills, but I also let the owner know I am going to train the course's staff for future growth, which of course is dependent on customer service. Although most owners, managers, and pros are not totally convinced we can bring in one thousand golfers, they are even more worried that we can. In some of the employees' eyes, these many golfers equate into a lot more work and no additional pay. Ten thousand additional rounds would mean working all day and taking their feet off the desk. No more SportsCenter reruns. Now they have to make coffee at 6:00 a.m. instead of 8:00 a.m. They have to pull thirty golf carts early in the morning instead of six, they have to get to the course by 6:00 a.m. instead of 8:00 a.m., they would have to actually put hot dogs on the warmer, they would have to stock the beer cooler, and so on, because after all, now the course would have a full tee-sheet.

Most managers and pros are making anywhere between $20,000 and $120,000 per year, but 80 percent are making between $28,000 and $60,000 per year. Some of the guys on the low end of the spectrum don't feel they are getting paid enough for the extra work, and some of the guys on the upper end feel as if the general public is beneath them and the course they represent. I am slightly amused when speaking with guys in the industry who have an elitist attitude. Remember, everyone needs to feel significant or important, and some golf pros and managers (as well as many other people in the world) meet this emotional need through their job title. Unfortunately, most of these guys don't have any skin in the game, so it's very easy for them to run off customers. Personally, I love being around the people who truly want to grow the game and share it with everyone, like the guy who introduced me to golf.

I was running a campaign for a health club in South Carolina around 1990. Up until that point in my life, I hated the idea of golfing. I've always loved and studied full-contact sports such as football, martial arts, and boxing. The idea of hitting a little ball around a field sounded painful to me. But I met a guy who worked at the club in Columbia who had just graduated from college, and he loved golf. This guy loved the game as much as I loved growing a business. When he spoke about golf, his eyes lit up, and you could just feel the energy all around him. Listening to him talk about the game was like listening to a kid telling a story about his first trip to Disney World.

This guy's future was set. He looked exactly like Tom Cruise and had one of the hottest tiny southern belles in South Carolina as his fiancée. This girl was smokin' hot and super sweet, and she came from an upscale family who owned one of the top-ten new golf courses in the South at the time. Every year, he organized a charitable golf outing that had a couple of hundred golfers' participation. He was a real stand-up guy who loved the game and wanted to share his passion with everyone.

Anyway, he and I got along great because he was extremely ambitious and wanted to learn sales and marketing. Every day, he would ask me to golf with him, and I just wasn't interested in wasting four hours of my day on golf. I had a negative association with the game because of my history with health club owners and managers who preferred to be on the golf course instead of in their clubs, taking care of businesses. But this guy was relentless, and one day, I gave in and said I would play a round with him.

I asked him what the best course in town to play was, and he told me, but with a disclaimer that we could never play it because it was closed to public play and only open to members—ultraexclusive. I told him to be ready to golf and we would play our first round at that country club the following week. He laughed his butt off, and then I could see the light come on, and he realized I was serious.

Since I am very competitive and think of myself as an athlete, I was not about to play a round with this guy without at least knowing the basics, so that evening, I set up a few lessons. Within a couple of lessons, I could hit the ball fairly well and was ready for my first round. I also called the country club and told them a friend and I were interested in visiting the club to enquire about membership (to be clear, I never said I was interested in joining), and as I knew they would, the membership director set us up with an early-morning tee-time as well as a complimentary breakfast for two. I don't remember the exact day, but I do know it was early in the week, like a Tuesday or Wednesday, because after a little research, I knew the course would be easier to get on since most golfers want to golf on the weekends.

For those of you who want to know how to get the biggest discounts on memberships and green fees, always join a golf course's loyalty program in the slowest times of the year. Golf courses, as well as all other membership-based businesses, roll out their best deals during their slow seasons. Never join a golf course in May, because you'll pay a premium. Most courses base their entire yearly budgets on April through September sales. Enquire in November, December, or January, when most courses are dead especially in the north and Midwest. Of course, the South and some parts of the Southwest are the total opposite. You want to enquire in June, July, or August when golfing in these regions. If you want to golf and want to avoid the premium green fees, go on a Monday through Thursday. These are the slowest days, and any time after 11:00 a.m. will be even better.

It was picturesque that early morning on the first tee-box. Light dew glimmered on the fairways and greens. At that very moment, I fell in love with the game of golf. I could now understand my friend's passion for the game. It was so much more than a sport; it was a lifestyle. We laughed and joked the entire time (mostly about how poorly I played). We literally had the course to ourselves, and it was one of the greatest memories of my life watching him explode with joy that morning having being able to share his love of the game with me. We finished our round and then had breakfast in the club's restaurant; this Tom Cruise look-alike was in complete disbelief the entire time. I explained to him golf courses have to raise revenue just like any other business, and since it is a member-based model, they too are always looking for new golfers. Even if a club has a waiting list, they will often entertain prospects to get them on the list. I also got lucky because there are not many golfers wanting to golf in South Carolina in the middle of the summer. This guy with the movie-star looks taught me a ton about the game of golf, and from that day forward, my eye was on the industry.

Another issue I would occasionally get pushback on was our 20 percent success fee. On the one hand, I was happy to hear someone voice his or her opinion rather than never bringing it up and choosing not to work with us because he or she didn't want to pay our commission. Most people are completely unaware of the man-hours, research, data, and so on that each campaign requires if done properly. One of the most important facts they fail to see is the course only pays MMC® 20 percent of the up-front cash and not one penny from the back-end revenue. Also, when factoring in the lifetime (potential revenue generated over ten or even twenty years) value of the golfer, which could be as much as $10,000 per golfer, the 20 percent that is paid to MMC® for acquiring that golfer is literally pennies on the dollar in relative terms. I would happily pay any company a $40 commission on every sale they made for me, especially if that sale came from a segment of the market I couldn't penetrate and the net value of that sale was a minimum of $600 and had the potential of being $10,000. Duh! It should be a no-brainer.

One of the challenges with owners is they don't understand the concept of *new money*. For some reason, they feel that all the golfers in their area are already their business even though they have never been engaged. For example, it's difficult for them to grasp that MMC® is locking up relationships with *consumers* who in some cases have never even held a golf club, much less are willing to commit to a traditional membership or loyalty program.

Think about it this way, if someone came to you and sat a box of money on your desk and said, "You and I are going to split this money that I have brought you eighty/twenty. You are going to receive the eighty percent, and I will only receive twenty percent even though it was I who brought the money in the door." Personally, if I owned the business I would make that deal all day long. Anyone willing to bring MMC® 80 percent of the up-front cash and 100 percent of the back-end revenue with no up-front fees and no out-of-pocket expenses is always welcome in my office.

On average, companies should spend about 10 percent of their gross revenue on marketing. I personally spend about 20–40 percent of MMC®'s gross revenue on marketing and research, because I know firsthand the enormous ROI that can be garnered from a properly engineered, executed, and managed marketing campaign. Growth is the bottom line for any business, especially for a business in an industry with an exodus of customers like golf. Our commission after factoring in projected back-end revenue raised by our campaign is around 4 percent. Then factor in the other costs, for example, printing, radio, newspaper, social media, banners, signs, and direct mail for the campaign, and the percentage may come up to an additional 4 percent, bringing the total marketing budget to 8 percent. But wait, now divide that number by two or three years relative to the duration of the introductory membership and now that number is more like 4 percent or even as low as 2.5 percent (depending on the success of the campaign) spent on the entire marketing budget. Now add in the additional revenue MMC® does not track, like buddy-referral green fees, range revenue, outing revenue, banquets, leagues, lessons, clinics, merchandise, club storage, locker fees, trail fees, annual cart passes, and social events, and that number goes to as low as less than 1 percent.

Where on earth can a golf course raise $250,000 in immediate cash, get as much as 500 percent growth in annual revenue with absolutely no money up-front or out-of-pocket cost, have absolutely no risk, have the venture completely pay for itself, and have it cost as little as 1 percent? Only with MMC®! When I came up with our success fee, I never dreamed anyone would ever think it was high. As I stated earlier, about thirty different people have their fingerprints on each project. And those people do not work for free.

The world is evolving every day, and if you are not moving forward you are going backward; it's just a fact. There is no such thing as staying where you are; if you are not growing, you're dying; if your business is not growing, it is dying. I am constantly advancing our research to provide the very latest and most up-to-date information I can for our clients. Unfortunately, research and development can get extremely expensive. I invest every dime possible back into MMC® to make our product better and better every day. I need to know I have done everything possible to provide my clients with the very best data, research, information, and assistance available to man. I am committed to a standard of excellence that most people and companies only talk about. My goal is to grow golf courses and grow the game. I never dreamed of being rich; I dream of making a difference in the world. My dream is to help people grow their business and be of service to the community and I accomplished this dream by transferring my love for the game to those who seldom play or have never golfed.

I am a lover of learning, and I believe a person's future is affected by two things: nature and nurture. Humans are born with certain characteristics (nature), and we develop certain characteristics through life experiences (nurture). Once I was given a personality profile based on my birth date by one of my secretaries, and the author used adjectives like steadfast, independent, honest, sensible, down to earth, imaginative, creative, hardworking, practical, business minded, enthusiastic, analytical, loyal, and truthful to describe me, and these are characteristics that I was not only born with but I nurture them daily. I know I was born to champion causes, serve others, and to do so honestly. I decided on the 20 percent success fee because of the cost I incur for each campaign not to get rich. I have been growing businesses for thirty-five years, and I love what I do.

My goal is to revolutionize the golf industry, and if I am going to realize that goal, I must change owners' ways of thinking when it comes to running a golf course. When faced with hard economic times, many owners and operators think of four ways to increase the revenue. The first thought is to raise membership dues on existing members or green fees on golfers. This is a huge mistake because the fallout of disgruntled members or golfers offsets the increased revenue. These golfers were probably just waiting for a logical excuse to quit anyway, and now you have handed it to them on a silver platter. This plan results in a loss of revenue more often than not. The only way this can work is if you are starting with a surplus of golfers and are prepared for the inevitable fallout.

Another ill-conceived plan to increase revenue is to force existing golfers to spend more in the profit centers. This too rarely works since consumers fall into spending patterns and develop buying habits, and it is extremely difficult to change these conditioned routines. Members and golfers are conditioned from the point of sale, and if you have not conditioned them to spend in the pro shop or in the restaurant, they never will. If you try to condition them a year or two down the road, your efforts may be perceived as greed by your loyal golfers and members. The delicate balance of conditioning and marketing will be important to your long-term growth.

For those of you old enough to remember the business prior to the 1980s, you know members of a golf course spent their money at the club. When members went out for a steak dinner, they went to the club.

When their children were married, the reception was held at the club. Birthdays and events were held at the club. If a member was seen out in a restaurant, other members would almost shame them for not supporting the club by eating at the club. These golfers were conditioned to support the club. Everything is completely different today, but the conditioning process can still take place; it just needs to be approached in other ways, and the last place to start is with preconditioned golfers.

Others believe the only way to survive this economic storm is to cut costs, and they usually start with cutting payroll, which in turn diminishes service and leads to unsatisfied golfers who eventually leave the course. The golf industry is a service industry. If we want to thrive (not just survive), we must provide unparalleled customer service. Members and guests alike want to feel like members, as if they belong, are welcome, and are appreciated. Remember that it costs six times as much to acquire a new golfer as it does to keep (service) an existing golfer, so do the math and provide the best customer service your budget will allow. No one has ever cut his or her way to prosperity by cutting customer service.

The best way to raise revenue and thrive in this or any storm is by bringing in new business and conditioning the new golfers' spending habits at the point of sale. This is exactly what MMC® does: we bring in new business from untapped segments, immediate cash, and increased revenue from profit centers, which equates to long-term residual income for the business. I have developed proven campaigns that target a group of individuals, which 99 percent of all other golf courses and marketing companies have neglected. I have had the luxury of traveling all over the United States and throughout the world, researching and compiling the most current data to develop a marketing strategy and a professional sales–training system designed specifically to support MMC®'s approach to ensure you dominate your market, not just secure market share. MMC® has invested millions of dollars in demographic and market research since 1989, eliminating the guesswork to provide our clients a proven method that works in the real world.

MMC®'s clients don't go out of business, and our clients' employees don't lose their jobs. You may ask why that is. It's because we capture new business from untapped segments and rebuild old relationships.

Whether it's the core and avid golfers or casual and nongolfers, all our customers have been selected through a thorough profiling criteria-based formula to assure the maximum ROI from our marketing efforts at a minimal expense. This is how you grow your golf course—not by raising members' dues, not by forcing golfers to buy unwanted products, and definitely not by cutting customer service.

As I am writing this book, the presidential campaign is going on between Hillary Clinton and Donald Trump. I am intrigued with the in-depth profiling they do on voters. Politicians have more demographic information on voters than most Fortune 500 companies do on their prospects. Politicians know what is at stake, and they know the value of every vote, which is why they put so much emphasis on demographics and profiling. Each candidate is aware on a daily basis of exactly which demographic is needed to win at whatever stage of the campaign they are in. Unfortunately, there are some golf-course owners who have absolutely no idea which demographic is going to give their business the financial freedom they so desperately long for. Profiling golfers is not a luxury; it is an absolute necessity!

In my opinion, course owners have been conditioned to spend very little on marketing and advertising and absolutely nothing on data or research. The reason for this is twofold. First, course owners never had to have a serious marketing budget because they were in the Field of Dreams business. Golf was golf, and if you wanted to golf, you had to be prepared to pay for it. The second reason is that when they did invest in marketing, it didn't work. The reason for this is that they relied on staff who had absolutely no experience with marketing other than what they had learned from other golf courses in their area, other industry people, or their fathers and grandfathers.

Most colleges or certificate programs let the student graduate with a passing grade of 70 percent. What kind of business can grow when the person responsible for growing the business only gets seven out of ten things correct? There is no way someone can successfully grow a business when they only get seven out of ten things right. One mistake can literally cost the owner tens of thousands of dollars. It reminds me of the age-old question, "What do you call a medical student who graduates last in his or her class? Doctor." When it comes to growing your golf course, you want someone who is at the top of their field, not someone who graduated last in their class.

This resistance to invest into marketing is another reason that I get pushback from time to time when it comes to direct mail. Our campaigns have been designed to completely pay for themselves, and the owner never comes out of pocket at any time. One of the challenges is when they see all this cash come in the door, the last thing they want to do is turn it loose and spend it on direct mail. In their naïveté, they fail to see the enormous value direct mail brings to the table, and by investing that revenue raised by the campaign back into direct mail, they can double, triple, and even quadruple their immediate cash within just a couple of weeks, not to mention that the same revenue will be duplicated for two to three years to follow. It's as though they don't comprehend the long-term residual returns on their investments, namely their back-end revenue. Understand that if you want to lock up relationships with casual and nongolfers, you must incorporate a profiled personalized direct-mail campaign or you will never engage them. It is stupidity to take the core and avid golfers out of the market without adding the other two segments to balance out the base. Through our research, we found that the only way to engage the casual and nongolfer segments is through personalized direct mail.

We have even experienced owners who get a quarter way through our campaign and then say they want to stop direct mail, even after it has brought in hundreds of golfers. I know this is just their fear of letting go of the cash in hand. They see bills on their desk, their bookkeeper is in their ear, and their wives are on their backs because now, for the first time, they have cash in hand, and everybody wants to get his or her share. I understand how tempting it is to pay past due chemical bills, taxes, mortgages, and so on, but if they are just patient and invest that cash back into direct mail, they will never be back in this situation again.

As I am writing this book, we are working with a nine-hole facility (I won't mention the state to protect the owner's identity). I called this owner one day, who was very interested in speaking with me because he was a member of a course where we (MMC®) had launched a campaign, and he had witnessed the enormous success. The club where he was a member did really well with our Cash campaign, and he knew it because he knew the owners of the other course very well and had grown up playing golf there as a kid. Now this nine-hole course owner wanted to know if my team could help him as well.

Although this owner was extremely interested, he was equally pessimistic. Speaking with him was both comical (because he had a great sense of humor) and torture because he was so stressed. Immediately, he let me know his personal and business lives were in shambles. He worked as a pro at a country club, which he referred to as his real job, and owned this little course, which was draining him financially and emotionally. He was putting everything he made from his real job into the business, and it still was sinking faster than the Titanic. The stress of the failing business was wreaking havoc on his personal life as well. He shared that he owed back taxes, had past due bills, and had numerous family problems mostly due to his failing business.

After a couple of conversations, we launched MMC®'s Cash campaign for his course, and every day he would let me know in no uncertain terms that it wasn't going to work. Initially, I projected we would easily sell five hundred introductory memberships, and he said it would never happen, but if it did, the money would be enough to save his business and relieve all his stress, and he would finally see a future owning the course. Within a couple of weeks of the campaign, we went to direct mail and edged closer and closer to the goal of five hundred. This owner never sent in a report, just e-mails with the numbers of the week, which sounded more like a random guess than an accounting. After two mail drops, we were around five hundred golfers, and I tried to get the owner to send in the wire for the third drop, but he politely refused.

He sent me an e-mail that basically informed me he had spent all the money paying his taxes and overdue bills, so he couldn't afford direct mail, but he wanted to continue selling the membership through the end of the year. Of course, I knew what he was doing, and I strongly advised against it. First, I knew he was underreporting his sales because we have a tracking system, which meant he was in far worse financial trouble than he had admitted. Second, he was now selling to only core and avid golfers, which was going to kill his business. He bartered for some print ads and other ads, thinking he could take shortcuts to save money. The problem is those free ads target only core and avid golfers, which will cannibalize his market for at least three years while destroying his brand, making it impossible for him to go back to his rack rates. Had he simply followed our instructions, he would have had the most successful nine-hole property in the Northeast. Unfortunately, he spent the money immediately instead of reinvesting it into the campaign, which would have yielded him one thousand or more golfers, doubled his cash in hand (cash collected at the point of sale), and brought in an additional $200,000 a year for the next three years.

Let's look at advertising with a little common sense for a moment. Since we are already talking about direct mail, I'll use it as an example. Let's say you are an owner in the middle of a campaign, like this owner was, and are faced with the decision to invest into more direct mail or not. This nine-hole property got a good response from direct mail, but let's use a poor-response rate of return from the first mail drop as an extreme example.

Let's say the first drop of twenty-five thousand pieces produced only one hundred additional golfers. Each golfer paid an average of $250. This means you have raised $25,000 in immediate cash from your first mail drop. Do you move forward, yes or no? My answer is absolutely yes, even if it is only one hundred new golfers! Why? Because the lifetime value of each golfer astronomically outweighs the cost of moving forward. The course needs to invest $10,000 to acquire one hundred new golfers; one hundred times $250 equals $25,000 in immediate cash. Twenty-five thousand dollars in immediate cash and you still have all the residual income from each golfer, which is an average of $200 per year per golfer times one hundred ($200 × 100), an additional $20,000 per year in back-end revenue. In short, that $10,000 investment turned into at least $55,000; that's a 450 percent ROI. This doesn't even take into consideration all the other potential revenue streams that will benefit from more traffic. Not to mention, these additional golfers will not be golfing at your competitor's course and increasing your competitor's revenue. So do you move forward, yes or no? Absolutely yes, even if it is only fifty new golfers!

Core and avid golfers will golf a hundred times a year if they can and will abuse the introductory membership. Not only that, but where is the owner going to get new golfers once he or she has sold all his core customers this inexpensive introductory offer? The owner can no longer penetrate the casual and nongolfer segments because he or she is no longer sending out the pieces designed for that course to the profiled list, which, by the way, he or she had already paid for. You cannot sell this introductory offer to only core and avid golfers because if you do—game over!

The saddest part about the nine-hole course from my point of view is not that the owner under reported his sales because if he had just talked with me I would have gladly worked something out. It's that the owner is a PGA member who had taken an oath to grow the game and to grow it with integrity. This was the perfect opportunity for him to do something really good for the game, his community, and his family, but he chose not to. If and when he goes out of business, his competitors won't say, "Damn, he should have done the campaign the way he was instructed by MMC®." Instead, they will say, "See, that cheap membership cost him his business." By not following through with the direct mail, the owner has no way of balancing out the books. One of the most basic lessons you learn in golf is follow through. Unfortunately, failure to follow through doesn't only kill your game, but it can kill your business as well.

This owner has given MMC® a glowing testimonial and has stated numerous times in his e-mails how we saved his business and his sanity, but all said and done, the campaign that saved him and could have been used as a catalyst to greatness will be blamed for the demise of the business. He is on cloud nine today because the cash is flowing like wine, but when the cash stops flowing, reality will hit and hit hard. The few hundred casual and nongolfers will start playing less, the core and avid golfers will decide it is better to walk instead of ride, and the beer sales will start to drop off because the core and avid golfers know how to beat the system. Course conditions will deteriorate with no money to keep up the maintenance and then this owner will realize the consequences of not following through. At this point, he will be looking for someone to blame, and I can guarantee you he won't look in the mirror.

It has been challenging over the past eleven years to get owners, managers, and pros to start thinking in terms of dollars (revenue) as opposed to rounds. Understanding marketing is a necessity and not an imposition. Targeting an untapped market is the only way to grow the game and a business. If there ever was a time to invest in marketing and branding, now is it. Don't try to wear all the hats. Hire professionals for the positions. Let people do what they do best and follow their lead. This industry is not overbuilt, and there is not too much inventory. There are more than enough customers if you just look past your core golfers.

CHAPTER 7

THE PROBLEMS THAT PLAGUE THE GOLF INDUSTRY

At this point of the book, you now know the three main reasons the golf industry hasn't been attracting new golfers or why very few courses, if any, have been successful in player development or in growing the game. Plain and simple: no marketing, inadequate marketing (no innovation), and focusing marketing efforts toward the wrong segments of the market. In this chapter, I want to show and share with you some of the things that have been slowly killing the golf industry, including my own unknowing contribution. I'll start by first throwing myself under the bus and disclose how I hurt half a dozen golf courses by my actions.

By 2007, I started rockin'. I was still launching campaigns for the health-club industry while I was building the golf division. I needed to clone myself so that there would be more of me because I couldn't possibly see how I could work at this pace much longer. I needed to leverage my time so that I could get off the road and have time to be innovative and creative to grow my own company. I wanted to revolutionize the golf industry, but I couldn't do it as a one-man band. I had this guy that worked with me in the health-club division for many years, and he was a real sharp salesman. By this time I had worked all the kinks out of the Cash campaign, and every campaign I was running for golf courses was knocking the cover off the ball, so I decided to bring him on board as a salesman to sell the campaign to course owners.

I had originally launched a campaign for a health club he owned, and it brought in $400,000 in cash in less than sixty days. Toward the end of the campaign, he asked me whether he could come to work for me. My first thought was, Are you kidding me? Here was a guy who wrote me one of the only two bad checks I had ever received from a client and now he wanted to represent MMC®. Fortunately for him, though, I knew club owners would love to work with him because he was a well-dressed, well-polished, well-educated, well-groomed, and likable guy with the right pedigree. This guy drove the right car and lived in the right house; he really looked and acted the part of a successful club owner. You would think he was the most successful club owner in the world when listening to his stories about his house at the beach, his weekends on the Cape, his ski vacations in Vermont, his golf trips to Florida, and so on. This guy was a natural-born salesman, that is, bullshitter—but of course I didn't know all of this when I brought him on board.

It is important to know what to look for when looking for a salesperson and then to expand on that search to find a salesperson who can live on the road. Being on the road takes a special breed of person, and it is extremely hard to find people who possess the sales skills who are also well educated, well spoken, well dressed, articulate, immune to rejection, willing to be away from their families for days or weeks at a time, and so on. Salespeople are normally not saddled with the stereotype of having great morals and values such as integrity, honesty, honor, and credibility (notice I didn't say "professional" salespeople). Most natural-born salespeople aren't known to be innovators or have the ability to pay attention to details either. On-the-road salespeople are special in their own way, but once in a great while, you'll find a diamond in the rough, and I was praying this man was an ole chunk of coal that could be polished into a diamond.

I needed someone I could program with my presentation, someone that could go on the road and visit clubs, freeing me up to be more innovative and creative and to grow MMC®. Of course, this was before the Internet's global acceptance as a tool for conducting business; otherwise, I would have simply done what I do now—put my presentations on video and upload them on our website and YouTube—which keeps MMC®'s message consistent while eliminating the risk of damage to our brand.

In life, and moreover in business, timing is everything, and this natural-born salesman entered my life at exactly the right time. I wanted help so badly that I started rationalizing how he could be just a mouthpiece, and since he had nothing to do with the campaign and was simply in the role of intermediary, he could be contained for the most part. I had already witnessed his natural ability for regurgitating every word I spoke back to me in the same conversation when I did his initial training for his club in Massachusetts, so I knew he could be programmed. He came up in the health-club business as a membership salesman, he knew the language of the industry, and he looked the part and knew the health-club business. He also knew MMC®'s Cash campaign from the owner's perspective since we had launched the campaign in his club, so he could relate well to other owners. All I had to do was teach him how to sell the campaign, and with his natural abilities to convince people, it would be an easy job for him. So I decided to give him a try.

The natural-born salesman lived in New England, so I assigned him the Northeast, which consisted of about eight states. I had him set up some appointments for him and me and then I flew up for a week to sell some clubs for him in his new territory. By the end of a week, I had sold a couple of club owners on the Cash campaign. He took to the sales presentation like a duck takes to water. Over dinner each night, he would recite back to me verbatim what I had discussed with the owners that day in our meetings. I was impressed and knew he would do very well if he just asserted himself. Being successful in the business of professional sales takes hard work; yes, you can con your way through life with the right look and a gifted tongue, but you will never be truly successful. No matter what, you have to have the drive and determination, study the craft, be willing to work hard, and put in the time. Unfortunately, most natural-born salespeople are allergic to hard work.

There are two schools of thought in business when it comes to getting your employees to perform: pain and pleasure (a.k.a., the carrot and stick). I like using the mule-and-cart metaphor to illustrate this point. You can motivate a mule to pull a cart with a carrot (pleasure) or with a stick (pain). Pain is an instant motivator, but it is a short-term tool because once you stop delivering the pain (whipping the mule), he stops pulling the cart. Pleasure, on the other hand, can be a long-term tool but a much slower process. The trick is to get the carrot out far enough to where the mule can smell the carrot but not close enough to where he can eat the carrot, so that he'll keep pulling the cart trying to get to the carrot. I screwed up because I rewarded my salesman with not only one carrot but thousands of carrots after he had pulled the cart only a couple of feet; he ate so well from one meal that it took him weeks before he ever thought about another carrot. Unknowingly, I turned my salesman into a hibernating bear. My heart was in the right place because I wanted to show people who worked with me that they had bright futures ahead if they just worked, and I was willing to reward them well to prove my commitment to their success.

I have always recruited people for specific jobs, jobs they love and possess the skill set to perform. This salesman was really a natural-born bullshitter, and that's why I made sure he stayed in sales. I did my best to accept him as he was, and since I knew him well after working with him for a few years, I made it a point to limit his access to clients' campaigns and kept him in an intermediary position. Within a few months of the salesman coming on board with MMC®, I started seeing the "salesman's" true colors and noticed he had a skewed view of the truth. The reason his first check to MMC® bounced was because his business was completely under water, and his creditors were about to seize everything he owned. He paid them with the initial cash to buy some more time; fortunately for him the campaign did very well. The salesman just didn't have the moral compass or work ethic to run a health club and eventually lost the business anyway, which is why he was so set on working with MMC®. No one (including me in the beginning) could ever think for a minute this guy's entire life was nothing but smoke and mirrors.

The only reason I let this guy continue representing MMC® was because he was an extremely likable guy. If you had a drink or dinner with him, you would love the guy, and most of our clients did. I would call some of his clubs just to introduce myself, and they would say nothing but great things about him. He was the perfect front man; while my team wrote the music and played the instruments and I conducted the orchestra behind the scenes, the salesman sat and held the client's hands and watched the show. As long as he was saying what I had taught him during the presentation and no more or less, he could charm the client and their staff with his personality. This guy just had the knack to make you comfortable, and since MMC® was running the campaign and pulling the strings behind the scenes, everything went smoothly 99.9 percent of the time. In Chinese philosophy, there is a saying: "There is always a little good in the really bad, a little bad in the really good; there is no right without wrong; there is no left without right; there is no east without west"—yin and yang. This guy was a people person; he just had some moral issues.

As I said earlier, this guy was just a salesman for MMC® and had nothing to do with the campaigns other than PR, which meant I felt safe having him sell our campaign to owners, so I decided to teach him the golf industry. At first, it was painful because although he golfed, he didn't know anything about the golf industry, so I had to start from scratch. It took me several years to teach him the business because he just didn't apply himself. As I said earlier, most smooth talkers are not hard workers, and he just didn't want to put in the work. After I had brought on a couple of golf industry guys (PGA members), he started paying more attention and came around because he started seeing nonsalesman selling the campaign. I sold a couple of courses in his area and let him do the PR; soon he found his confidence. During his time representing MMC®'s golf division, he was the front man for about eighteen projects, who ran our Cash campaign in the Northeast region.

After a few years, I was getting tired of babysitting him, though, and wanted him out of the company. I tried several times to get the salesman to leave on his own, but he didn't want to go; he hung on to MMC® like a tick on a dog, and I have a serious flaw (or characteristic trait)—I'm as loyal as a dog. He lost the rights to his original agreement due to countless breaches several years ago, but I allowed him to stay on as an independent contractor because his wife called me and pleaded with me, citing her family's welfare depended on MMC®. Finally, in January 2015, I couldn't take his lies, excuses, and BS anymore and decided not to renew his independent contractor's agreement and to cut all ties with him.

On February 16, 2016, MMC®'s office received a complaint from a course manager in Massachusetts regarding this "salesman." The manager informed me one of MMC®'s past representatives had convinced the owner to run a second campaign in March 2015, allegedly representing himself as still being affiliated with MMC®. I was told this natural-born salesman proposed an online promotion and that he, as the consultant, would collect all the revenue from the golfers' new memberships and would then send the owners their percentage of the revenue. The owners claimed they had been conned and had never received payment. In their attempts to collect, they received nothing but excuse after excuse for almost a year, yet this salesman allegedly was still deducting payments from their golfers' bank accounts and credit-card accounts. Since this salesman represented MMC® in the past, we felt it was our responsibility to contact everyone in his previous sales territory and let them know he had not been affiliated with MMC® since January 2015.

MMC® ran a campaign for this Massachusetts course in 2011 and raised more than $125,000 in immediate cash. It was easy to understand how this alleged con had merit to materialize since this course's ownership already had confidence in MMC®'s marketing campaigns and ethics, due to their previous experience with MMC®. This salesman was the course's contact person, so it was easy for the course owner to associate trust with the salesman and, therefore, be easily convinced of his future representations of a new campaign (false or otherwise).

The term con man is derived from the word confidence. A con man gains your confidence (trust) with a scheme or transaction in which you receive the better part of an exchange and then convinces you to trust him again at a later time, when of course you get the short end of the stick, and it is normally shoved up your butt. The hardest part of a con is gaining the confidence of the mark (victim), but once the foundation has been laid, all that is left is the execution of the con. MMC®'s Cash campaign is so successful it was the perfect foundation, making it easy for one of our former representatives to use the Cash campaign's previous success, as well as MMC®'s good name, to gain the trust and confidence of one of our past clients.

Over the next several months, my office received half a dozen complaints about this salesman and his con game. He had contacted several of MMC®'s previous clients, trying to sell them on this new promotion. Several courses called our office and informed us the salesman was claiming to do an online e-mail campaign, using, of course, the only thing he knew—MMC®'s intellectual property and materials.

When someone comes to you claiming he or she will buy or sell you an e-mail list, get as far away from him or her as fast as possible. As I have stated earlier, e-mails are an opt-in-only list. It is unethical to buy e-mail lists, and using them can kill your online presence and, in some cases, get you slapped with a hefty fine or imprisoned. This salesman knew all this from working with MMC® and had heard me condemning the practice numerous times when course owners requested us to buy an e-mail list for their course. The salesman claimed he was buying the e-mail list for $4,200 and sending out the purchased e-mails along with the e-mails from the course's e-mail list. This is a common con well known in the digital world. What he really did was only send out e-mails to the course's existing list. He not only collected thousands in ill-gotten commissions but also billed the course for two nonexistent e-mail lists totaling $8,400. This salesman allegedly conned the owner out of about $20,000. This was a very easy con for him not only because he used MMC®'s previous campaign as the foundation of his con but also because he was able to capitalize on these owners' hunger for cheap e-mail marketing. As I said earlier, owners hear about these cheap marketing campaigns, and in an attempt to save a nickel, they throw away a dollar.

Out of about six complaints, one course really stood out because during our investigation, my team discovered the past client actually had been informed this guy was no longer with MMC® in the middle of his "e-mail" campaign (scam), but the course owner liked working with the salesman so much that he chose to continue working with him anyway. When I called the owner after this truth was uncovered, the owner confirmed my team's discovery and said he couldn't help himself because the salesman was so believable and likeable. This is one of the many problems with having representatives. People, including customers, like people like themselves and get blinded by their personal relationships. The worst thing was this course brought in $316,000 in the first half of the MMC®'s Cash campaign that the course owner originally ran with MMC® a year before. He stopped after only two mail drops because he was afraid his course would be too busy. The following year, after the salesman's IC (Independent Contractor) agreement had been terminated by MMC®, the owner called the salesman on his mobile, thinking he was still with MMC® and told him he wanted to relaunch the campaign because he still had plenty of room for more golfers (which is exactly what we had told him the previous year). The salesman told the owner it was better to do an e-mail campaign instead of finishing the direct-mail campaign because it was much cheaper than direct mail—which was part of the con, of course because he was setting the "trust me I'll save you money" hook. This owner still had thirty-five thousand pieces of mail sitting in the warehouse, already paid for. All he had to pay was the postage and handling, and he could have earned another $300,000 or more in immediate cash and another $300,000 plus per year for the next two years—he lost $900,000 or more all because he liked the "salesman," even when he knew the salesman had stolen our property, lied about the direct mail, given a million off-the-wall excuses as to why the "new" campaign was failing, and had even lied to the course owner about his current status with MMC®. Instead of making a million dollars in ninety days with MMC®, he spent six months chasing an alleged criminal for $20,000.

The owner should have picked up the phone and called MMC®'s home office the minute things started sounding shady, but to his detriment, he made a conscious decision to continue believing the salesman even after catching him in numerous lies—karma.

The funniest thing now that all this is behind us is that two of the six courses that had called MMC® to help them get their money back from the natural-born salesman came back to us (after they did get their money back) asking for our help once again. In one of the cases, the owner took the new information we gave him and tried to launch the campaign on his own, and the other worked with us and underreported the sales by more than half and gave me one lame excuse after the other. I had to laugh at myself because I was so worried about our brand that I was willing to go to the end of the earth to help these owners and when I did all I got was a clear understanding why they both liked the natural-born salesman so much—people like people like themselves.

Over twenty-five years, MMC® has had several representatives, and luckily, this was only the second ex-rep who had allegedly done anything criminal like this. One other time, many years ago, one of our

Independent Contractor's contract was terminated, and he too went to a previous client, got her to pay him a $2,500 advance for a new campaign he was peddling, and then skipped town. Once my team was informed, just as we did in all the above cases we did everything possible to help the club get their money back. This ex-rep had been with MMC® only a few short months and had worked with only two clubs, so he was easily contained. Other than those two incidents, we have never heard of any other alleged theft or fraud from course owners concerning any of our other ex-ICs. I am not saying some guys didn't steal a few of our ideas and sales presentation, trying to start their own companies—that happens every few years or so—but their efforts always fail due to their ignorance of the total picture. They have the sales presentation down because that, and only that, is what we taught them, but when the rubber meets the road, they always crash and burn.

The biggest and greatest threat to the golf industry as a whole is not alleged criminals like this salesman—it's copycats. Criminals always get caught, and in the worst-case scenario, they may affect a dozen golf courses, whereas copycats are far more dangerous because their thievery spreads like an undetected virus throughout the industry, killing every business in its path. Unfortunately, I see this way too often in the golf industry.

I'll use the natural born salesman again to illustrate the damage a copycat can do to a golf course. After learning of his alleged fraud, my team found his website, which was just a blatant rip-off of MMC®'s website. He actually put MMC®'s clients' testimonials on the site but changed them to reflect his company. We called our clients and told them what he had done, and they called him, demanding he take their names off his website, which he did immediately and then took down the entire website a few days later. About a year has passed since we heard anything about the natural-born salesman, and then just the other day I got a call from a course owner who told me the salesman was back to his old tricks again and has started a new marketing company using a three letter abbreviation similar to MMC® and is still using mmc in his e-mail address.

Unfortunately we can't stop him from using "mmc" in his email address because he is not using MMC®'s domain, that is, *@mmctoday*.

com. He just uses an email with his name and "mmc" at the end from a free email dot net (.net) provider. Another good lesson for all business owners, if you have anyone represent your company always give them a company owned email address and insist on them using it for all business related correspondence. This way, if they are terminated they can't fool people into believing they are still in good standing with your company. Hindsight is definitely twenty-twenty.

On his new website, he claims he has many offices and a huge staff, has worked with many courses, has over fifty years of experience (the guy is only fifty-plus years old), which of course is all taken straight from MMC®'s website, but in reality, this guy works out of the trunk of his car using his wife, kids, and dog as his "staff." He also put numerous course testimonials on his website, again something he borrowed from MMC®. The only difference is when we called his testimonials, none of them knew him or his company. He must have randomly selected course names, addresses, websites, and e-mails to make it look legitimate and written testimonials to himself on their behalf. Everything this guy does is smoke and mirrors.

I know what some of you readers are thinking right now: "Who cares? That's your company's problem. What does that have to do with me or the golf industry?" First, it has a lot to do with you. Let's say you hire a copycat like the salesman because of his golden tongue and beautiful website that says all the right things, but you have no idea he is a fraud and has stolen every word, phrase, and promise; in short, he takes your last hope along with your last dollar. This scenario sounds bad enough, but wait—the snowball has just begun its journey downhill.

Next, it starts affecting all of the competitors, because now all of the core and avid golfers are playing cheap golf, and there are no more green fees to be garnered. In a year or so, the real affects start to hit his victim and now the business is forced to close. The three or four hundred golfers who prepaid their memberships now have been duped and have nothing but bad things to say about the owner. All of the staff members lose their jobs. The owner of the course loses everything he and his family has worked for all of their lives, including their reputations. The community suffers the loss of another business as well as green space that will now be developed into track housing or even worse...strip malls. The industry suffers one more disappointment trying to explain why one more golf course has closed. The game loses more traction because of the bad publicity, and thousands of my beloved casual and nongolfers in that market will never get to be introduced to the game I love so dearly. Copycats like the salesman are not just my problem—they are everyone's worse nightmare.

I am truly sorry for introducing that salesman to the golf industry, but in my defense, I did everything I could to inform every golf course in the United States immediately that he was no longer with our company. I can't control everyone who comes in contact with MMC®'s products and services, but because of this ex-representative, we at MMC® had to make drastic changes in the way we do business. We no longer have outside reps or ICs, other than one who has been with us for over ten years. Other than him, all our reps are now either employed by MMC® or have left the company. All of MMC®'s presentations are now on video and uploaded on our website (www.golfmarketingmmc.com) for our prospects to view at their leisure. If a customer wants to speak to one of our representatives, all he or she has to do is call our office at 904-217-3762 (toll free 877-620-8135) or e-mail me at chuck@mmctoday.com.

Copycats are everywhere in the golf industry, and some are far more destructive than the salesman if you can believe that. Something as small as a competitor copying your ideas can ruin a market within months. It's like high blood pressure—a silent killer. I know you can remember a time when you launched a campaign and the following month you saw your competitor launch the same exact campaign. When all the courses in your area are running exactly the same offer, targeting the exact same segment of the market and the same demographics, with the same price point, the piece of the pie for each course just gets smaller and smaller. The first course to be seated at the table always gets the largest piece, and the last course to be seated is left with just the crumbs. The main reason each consecutive course gets a smaller slice is not because all the prospects are gone from the market; it's because the quality of the campaign is deteriorating with each copy. Think about it logically: each golf course is in a different geographical area, and since most golf courses pull from at least a twenty-mile radius, each course is going to have some (if not the largest) portion of its population that does not overlap with the other courses in the area running the same campaign, leaving a large portion of the population untouched, which would lead you to believe the offer should still pull well.

Wrong! It is not only that the offer stops pulling; it is that the details of the campaign have been diminishing from course to course. Just like when you photocopy something over and over, it gets less visible with each copy unless you change the ink cartridge. The same applies when someone is copying a promotional offer; it gets weaker and weaker each time it is copied. This is because each course gets further and further away from the original design and implementation. In short, too many cooks in the kitchen are going to spoil the stew.

Forget what your neighbor is doing because more than likely, he or she is doing what his or her neighbor did, and they are both doing it wrong. Copying your competitor's marketing or business model is a recipe for disaster. Growing a business is similar to playing chess; you must be thinking at least three moves in advance of your competitor, not following behind him or her. If you continue playing the copying game or follow the leader—you will always lose.

I'll use MMC®'s Cash campaign as an example: When competitors of courses partnering with MMC® see our Cash campaign being launched for our client's course, inevitably one or two of the competitors will try and copy the campaign within a few months because no matter how great their courses are—they will definitely feel the pain of MMC®'s Cash campaign. Competitors assume (ass-u-me is when you make an ass of you and me) they know everything there is to know about the campaign when all they know is the price point and what they heard through the grapevine from either their golfers or colleagues in the industry. Because of their ignorance and desperation, they launch a hybrid of our campaign in their course, ruining their business and market forever, because all they have done is give a cheap membership to core and avid golfers who would have paid the course's published rates had they just been engaged properly.

But wait, the situation gets even worse because now another competitor on the other side of their market sees the first competitor running what appears to be a similar campaign and copies what he or she can, which is now down to about 2 percent of the original campaign because the first competitor cut corners to save money and implemented only half of what he or she copied. By the time the fifth course copies the abbreviated version of the Cash campaign, all that is left of the original campaign is the price point. It is this perversion of MMC®'s Cash campaign (focusing solely on the price point) that is contributing to the financial ruin of some golf courses. Unfortunately, the word will get out that ABC course ran a promotion for such-and-such price and the failure will be unfairly linked to MMC®'s campaign when MMC® had absolutely nothing to do with the promotion.

Under normal circumstances, if a campaign yields three hundred golfers, you should throw a party and celebrate. Three hundred golfers from a campaign like MMC®'s Cash campaign are considered a huge flop, because those three hundred golfers most likely came from your core market. Most media, including social and e-marketing platforms, target your core market and preexisting customers. If you do not incorporate a consumer profile list based on specific criteria, identifying the consumer's spending habits, designed to recognize consumers who have purchased within the golf categories within the past twelve to eighteen months but have no other ties or links to playing golf, with a message tailored to their psychological needs delivered via personalized direct mail, which is put directly in their hands—you're hanging yourself with the little rope you "borrowed".

When courses put their ads in newspapers, on the radio, and on social-media platforms, the only people who are paying attention to them are the consumers who are already paying attention and are presently a part of the course's prospect community. There are three important factors novices fail to realize. First, almost every generation gets its news and information from different media and platforms. Second, anyone with a great facility who is willing to drop his or her pants (rates) can easily capture the core- and avid-golfer segments of the market. Third, the only way to grow a business is to acquire the customers from segments or groups that are not being engaged because these segments actually grow the business as well as the industry. If a course is not tapping into new markets and segments, they are only recycling golfers.

"Cherry pickers" is a term I use to describe those people who target the low-hanging fruit and leave all the other (more difficult to reach) fruit on the tree. They do exactly the same with prospects. They cherry-pick a promotion, a website, a presentation, a campaign, or whatever else they can get their hands on to get the quick and easy information to sell the easiest prospects, but because of their greed, laziness, and lack of innovation, they inevitably leave 80 percent of the fruit on the tree. Talk about leaving money on the table; these "geniuses" are like bank robbers who empty out the tellers' drawers but leave the safe untouched. They naïvely think they are cherry-picking a campaign for the good stuff, when all they do is ruin the fruit for themselves as well as everyone else. MMC®'s Cash campaign is designed to grow the business, not to give golf away!

Copycats and cherry pickers are everywhere. We at MMC® deal with them on a daily basis. Many golf-marketing companies are plagued with laziness and lack of innovation as well. It is difficult to keep coming up with new ideas to improve your product unless you have unwavering focus and are willing to invest in research, study, and work. Unfortunately, most of these companies' leadership teams just don't have the innovative spirit to come up with new ways of growing a business, so they troll other companies' websites, blogs, vlogs, presentations, videos, and so on in hopes of finding new ideas. I even had a competitor copy the description off one of our videos and use it for his own video description, but like an idiot, he forgot to take MMC®'s name off the description when uploading it to YouTube. Companies like these are legendary for plagiarizing other people's ideas and claiming them as their own. The only impact companies like these have on a business is negative.

Ex-reps and competing marketing companies are not the only guilty parties when it comes to theft in the golf industry. I only using my personal experiences as examples for this book because I don't want to throw anyone under the bus publicly, but I have seen far worse happen to golfers and course owners alike. I speak with owners on a regular basis who have experienced similar deplorable scenarios as well. In the early days of MMC®'s golf division, one of my guys and I were making a presentation to an owner who had a little management company that managed six or seven courses, the majority of which were in Texas. After a few conversations, he got us on the phone with his team, and within a few minutes, I could tell he was just fishing for information. After we had made our presentation to his team, it was evident he was planning on stealing our ideas so that he could try to launch an imitation of our campaign without paying us.

Sure enough, we monitored their courses' advertising, and within days they launched a campaign—via social media and newspaper—with the information they had garnered from our presentation. I am extremely happy to say it failed miserably. My staff came back to me a couple of weeks later and told me the management company had stopped the campaign. We had originally projected those courses to raise well over a million dollars in up-front cash and several million dollars in back-end revenue (and they would have easily surpassed those conservative projections), but due to the greed and unscrupulous morals of the management company's leadership, a couple of those courses tanked within a few years, and it was the owners of the courses who suffered—not the ownership of the management company. Since they were just the management company (a hired hand who receives their monthly fee no matter what), they walked away untouched.

Another example of this is when a manager/pro in Washington State called us for some information (sound familiar?), and after a few thirty-minute conversations, we didn't hear from him again. A few weeks later, my team informed me he was running (ruining) a campaign with the information we had shared with him in our presentation. He visited our website a few times and watched some videos and then came to the conclusion he was now an expert with his newly acquired education. Remember, out of all the information he received (all in all, at least several dozen bits of valuable information between the phone calls, videos, blogs, vlogs, etc.) in doing his homework, the only thing he remembered was the price point, and he even screwed that up in an attempt to hide his theft.

He posted an ad on the course's FB page and then recorded a message on the course's voice mail. On their voice mail, he recorded the wrong URL address to the course's website. He also said on the recording that the promo offer was a two-year pass for 2016 and 2017 for $150, but on their FB page, it read $150 per year. Inconsistency makes people feel like they can't trust you—case in point. These were just two extremely simple ads, and he had completely screwed them up in all his infinite wisdom. Can you imagine how bad this campaign went from that point onward? There are a thousand things you must know when launching a campaign like this, and this genius got everything wrong.

He probably sold a couple of hundred memberships despite his own stupidity, but he will bankrupt the course in the process. This campaign is designed for the casual and nongolfer. Yes, he will sell a couple of hundred memberships to his current golfers and feel like a hero for a couple of months, but then it will hit him (and his owners) that he cannibalized his future green fees and memberships. He brought no new golfers to the table and completely devalued his product and now will be known as that course where you can play unlimited golf for one (or is it two? I'm confused by the advertisements) year(s) for $150. If you're too ignorant to tell time, don't try to build a watch!

As I am writing this book, I had a case similar to the last example arise with an owner who called me from the Midwest. He claimed to have one of the top-ten courses in the country but could not get golfers to commit or even play his course. He blamed everyone from his ex-partners, ex-pros, ex-employees to even his members. I remember a line someone once told me: "If everyone around you is the problem, maybe the problem is a little closer than you thought—you." This couldn't have been any truer for this owner. He called and e-mailed me every other day, wanting to know more and more about MMC®'s Cash campaign. I could see he was fishing for information, so I stopped him in his tracks and told him there would be no more conversations until we received a signed contract. A few days later, the contract came, and the phone calls and e-mails started coming in faster than ever. One day I got a call from the owner, and he asked if I would talk to a friend of his for a few minutes. A guy picked up the phone, introduced himself, and explained he was a well-known name in the golf industry and hosted a local radio show.

Immediately, the radio host started fishing for information on our campaign and wanted us to design something for his show and for a golf convention that was coming up. I told him in no uncertain terms I was not interested because our campaign was not designed to attract core and avid golfers and that its sole function was to target casual and nongolfers to grow the business. The more I spoke against the idea of promoting our program on his radio show or at the convention (which are both targeting core and avid golfers), the more this host persisted, finally ending with "What does the owner pay MMC® on other business revenue other than your introductory membership?" I informed the host that MMC® only gets paid on what our campaign brings in the door and nothing else. I knew he was thinking of convincing the owner to advertise it anyway, but at this point I was tired of trying to protect the owner, because he seemed set on partnering with the radio host no matter what I said.

We were supposed to launch the campaign that Friday but could not get a hold of the owner or his manager all weekend. On Tuesday or Wednesday of the following week, we got an e-mail from the owner claiming we should raise our price point up fifty dollars because that was what he did when the campaign "accidently" got leaked at the convention and announced on the radio. Wow, my suspicions were spot on. This host convinced the owner to promote the membership to core and avid golfers and, by doing so, killed his market and the campaign. When I shared my disappointment, the owner proudly said, "But we sold almost two hundred memberships."

I replied, "Of course you did, and you will sell another three hundred, but then you'll be done, and by then you might as well go straight to bankruptcy court, because all you accomplished was selling an introductory membership to core and avid golfers, who don't spend in the profit centers and will now be golfing for the next one, two, or even three years for a minimal prepaid fee. Great job, genius!"

This owner desperately tried to get us to move forward with the campaign for the next several weeks because "his" promotion was starting to crash and burn, and he started seeing his (financial future) life flash before his eyes like someone who was about to die in a horrific crash. There was absolutely no way I was going to partner with someone who conducted business in such an unethical way, and I was not about to let MMC®'s name be associated with this train wreck. In our initial discussions he went on and on about his dream and committed to provide the best product available to high-end consumers wanting to golf at one of the finest golf properties in the United States, and had he followed my strategy, that dream would have become a reality, but now he had completely destroyed his dream, market, and financial future all because he wanted to charge fifty dollars more per membership to prove his point. This genius received fifty dollars more from three hundred people ($15,000) but lost more than two million dollars in up-front cash and back-end revenue. Guys like this will cut off their nose just to spite their face. I personally prefer to be successful more than always "right."

One of the other huge mistakes courses often make is that they design a losing package. They either give everything away or don't give enough to make the campaign successful. Finding the right balance between value and investment is paramount to the success of any campaign. It took me years of managing countless campaigns to understand the dynamics of the product well enough to maximize the return while eliminating the downside. Having the ability, or inability, to adjust on the fly can make or break any campaign.

This reminds me of another course I recently launched a campaign for, who was a two-time client of ours in the past but now had contacted one of our vendors for pricing. The vendor immediately called us, and I called the owner of the course to see how I could be of assistance. This owner is a great guy. When we spoke, he confirmed my suspicions and told me point-blank he didn't want to pay our 20 percent success fee. He informed me that he had kept all the materials and could just tweak them with a new expiration date and save the commission. Ignorance is truly bliss.

I understood his thought process because he was definitely not the first course to think this, but he was the first owner to go to our vendors and be truthful about his intentions, and I had to respect his honesty, even if the idea was ludicrous. I immediately went into the numerous reasons he would be better off having MMC® launch the campaign for him, but he wasn't having it because he was dead set against paying our commission. At this stage, he thought he knew enough about our Cash campaign to run (ruin) it on his own. The bottom line was he just wanted to avoid paying our success fee. As I stated earlier, this owner had run two campaigns with MMC®, which were both managed by different salesmen; the first guy was someone who had left the company a few years ago to work for a management company, and the other one was the guy who was still with MMC®, who managed the owner's project a year and a half ago. This course did very well with us both times grossing well over $350,000 in up-front cash and selling more than fifteen hundred memberships, which means he probably did another $1 million plus in back-end revenue.

Because of the owner's history with MMC®, I wanted to help him with his renewal program. I also wanted to help him for personal reasons as well; for example, save the integrity of the campaign and gather some important data. Besides, he still had two drops of mail totaling almost thirty-five thousand pieces plus his mailing list that he had paid for during the last campaign, which he never used because he too thought he had sold too many introductory memberships the previous year. I didn't want him to lose the money he had already spent, and I knew direct mail was his only hope of getting anywhere near his goal. The funny thing was that he didn't even remember the inventory he already had until I brought it to his attention. He was not starting out very well, to say the least. In that one minute, I saved him several thousand dollars in expenses and probably made him $200,000 in new sales from the direct mail. Simple mistakes can kill a business.

I wanted to conduct a little research on why some clients who have partnered with us and run our Cash campaign, who also had the materials as well as the training, still did such a poor job with renewals and the campaign when they launched the campaign on their own. In twenty-five years, we have never done a campaign for free, because it costs us so much in hard cost to implement and manage each project. This was different though; most of the work had been done, and all of the data had been purchased, so I chalked this project up to customer service and research. I wasn't going to launch the campaign for him, neither was I, nor was my staff, going to manage the campaign. I told the owner I would help him with his renewal program so that he could raise the money to send out his remaining direct mail, but after that, he would be on his own. I knew from experience that if I had left him on his own from the start, he (or anyone else) would screw the campaign up royally, but I wanted to be able to prove my theory beyond a shadow of a doubt, and since he was insistent on doing it on his own, who was I to say no?

I agreed to get this course through its initial e-mail campaign, which would be sent to its current members for renewal, and which would easily raise enough money to pay for the postage and handling for its two remaining drops. I knew MMC® couldn't afford to do all the work and buy all the data that went into a new project, but even with the limited time and manpower I would be devoting to the project, the owner would be far better off than had I not gotten involved at all. I, of course, would be compensated by knowing I helped a client beyond what was expected of MMC®, and I would learn firsthand how much an owner really knows about the campaign after having it launched at his course—twice.

I asked the owner to send me the e-mail he had planned on sending out to his members so that I could tweak it. Sure enough, when I got the e-mail, it was dreadful. First, it was an old e-mail we had designed several years ago and no longer used because there had been numerous improvements and revisions. I am constantly changing, updating, and reinventing ways to get better responses from all media and platforms. I have an appetite for knowledge that will never be fulfilled, and I thrive on learning and growing, which means our products are always evolving.

As I have said numerous times, we are extremely fortunate, because we've worked with hundreds of properties and have the advantage of learning from our experiences. I am always looking for ways to make our advertising pull better. I twist, turn, add, and delete words, phrases, and paragraphs daily to see if there is a negative or positive effect on the response. Sometimes it may be a single word that makes a huge difference. For example, this owner decided to change the original headline and insert his own. The new headline of this owner's e-mail was, "Back by popular demand." From a novice's perspective, this was a good headline, but from a professional's perspective, this was a disastrous headline. By advertising that this price point was back by popular demand, it left it open for the golfer and prospect to assume this offer could and probably would be offered again, so why not wait until the next time? And wow! What does that do to the brand? That course would never be able to increase its rates.

Another problem was members would have already seen that e-mail and subject line and would have just deleted it. Also, the original e-mail we wrote for this course was not a renewal letter for his members but a letter for his entire e-mail list. Hence, the email subject made no call to action to get current members to renew their memberships today. In fact, in most e-mails, we discourage current members from migrating over, so we down sell the opportunity. Because this was the first e-mail MMC® had sent out in a previous campaign, the owner assumed it should be the first e-mail he should send out in this campaign. Wrong! He needed to renew as many of his current golfers as possible before launching to the public, even though their memberships would not be expiring for another five months. By offering the membership to the present members first, he would make them feel special, which would assist in getting them to renew now and stay loyal to the course. The way he had it written, the current members, as well as all other prospects, would have thought to themselves there was no hurry to make the decision. In addition to all the other mistakes, he chose to use the same price point as his previous campaign, which was another catastrophic mistake.

Previously the campaign had run for three months (ninety days), which most of his current members would remember, since the campaign had been rolled out twice before. People are procrastinators by nature; if they think they can put something off until tomorrow, they will, and we all know "tomorrow never comes." Once something is out of sight, it will be out of mind. His members would then forget about the offer, since his season was coming to an end, and they wouldn't think about it again until next golf season.

His plan was to use old e-mails, newspaper ads, and mail pieces, as well as the old price point. He was forgetting a basic fact of the human psyche, and that is, if your brain assumes it has seen something before, it will save energy by compartmentalizing that information and storing it as "seen that, done that." This is why almost every course that tries to renew golfers on its own has renewal rates of about 40 to 60 percent. But when a course calls MMC® to manage its renewal program, the percentage normally goes up to 80 percent renewal or more.

In our conversation about the e-mail, he confirmed he was second-guessing himself about the headline and had never considered the other dozen things I had pointed out that would have dramatically diminished his response. In closing, he asked if it was ready to be sent out, and I replied, "Yes, but make sure you send it out after nine a.m."

He asked, "Why is that again?" and I told him people try to clear their e-mails that come in the night before as soon as they get behind their desk so that they start their day afresh, but after 9:00 a.m., they actually welcome the e-mails and tend to read them. He said, "Oh yeah, I remembered hearing something about that from the last campaign." This little tidbit literally made this owner's open rate go up by at least 25 percent.

I chuckled to myself because had I not mentioned it, he would have never remembered it and would have made another costly novice mistake. Some people say, "Don't sweat the little things," but I say, "It's the little things that matter most."

I followed up with him about a week later and asked if he was ready to send in his money for the postage and handling. He was shocked and said the last time we sent the money in was after two weeks. I said, "Yes, you did, but then you were not on a tight schedule like you are now, nor did you have the attention of the two thousand golfers that you have now." Had he known what he was doing, he would have already had two more e-mails out to different lists, as well as a few newspaper ads and radio spots running. Instead, he had sent only the one e-mail and now was at least four weeks behind in the campaign. Yes, only a week had passed, but he needed to have a bunch of things in place by this time if he was going to stay on schedule, and since he had no idea of how to manage the campaign, he was a minimum of four weeks behind already.

This course would end up bringing in about $125,000, which would consist of about five hundred renewals and a couple of hundred new golfers by doing his renewal campaign on his own (but still using our profiled list, direct-mail piece, my coaching, and all our materials). By letting a nickel get in the way of a dollar (avoiding MMC®'s success fee), he would fall far short of his goal and would have squandered a perfect opportunity to raise more than $300,000 in immediate cash and an additional $300,000 a year over the next three years in back-end revenue. Yes, he would have paid MMC® $60,000, but we would have brought him an additional $175,000 in up-front cash plus the back-end revenue, meaning his decision to cut corners cost him more than a half a million dollars. Personally, I would pay $60,000 to get a 1,000 percent return (in ninety days) all day long. Remember, this half a million is not an arbitrary number; we have worked with this course twice and know the numbers well.

I coined the expression "The Tao (pronounced Dao) is in the details." The Tao is a Chinese term that means the path or the way, and the path to success is in the details. This owner had saved all the materials, had worked with MMC® twice, and he and his staff had been thoroughly trained by three different people, but he still made a hundred (if not hundreds) novice mistakes, all of which or any one of his mistakes cost him thousands of dollars. MMC®'s campaigns have four phases, and each phase has at least a hundred different working parts, and each working part has at least a dozen details that must be included or you will feel the pain in your results. The sad thing is when owners do this, they sometimes blame the campaign, but the fault doesn't lie in the product; it lies in the implementation.

A campaign of this magnitude consumes hours upon hours of our staff's time, which, in my experience, most owners and managers don't have, that is, qualified marketing staff or extra time. Most owners as well as their staff are already wearing too many hats, yet some owners want to saddle their staff or themselves with this enormous responsibility of growing the business. It is my bet that you the owner are constantly disappointed with the performance of your business, and now you are going to add even more burden by assigning this marketing campaign to a first-timer. Even if the staff member was a tenth-timer, it wouldn't make a difference. A successful campaign demands hours and hours of personnel to monitor social media, gather data, conduct surveys, run competitive overviews, and so on. Any given campaign launched by MMC® has a minimum of thirty people's fingerprints on the project.

There is an old saying in the legal world: "A man who is his own lawyer has a fool for a client and an idiot for an attorney." Forget for a minute that I am the one saying this, and think logically for a second. If you own a course, you get one shot at running (ruining) a campaign of this magnitude; if you, your employee, or whoever you hire makes only one mistake (out of a thousand possible mistakes), you could literally screw up your course's financial future or even worse—bankrupt the business.

I am a firm believer in people asking themselves good questions. Ask yourself this: Have you or your staff ever launched a million-dollar campaign? I am absolutely sure the answer is no. Then why on earth would you think in your wildest imagination you or your staff would be qualified to launch and manage MMC®'s Cash campaign? Even with all the information I have shared with you in this book of things to do and examples of things not to do, you have less than 20 percent of what goes into one of our campaigns and absolutely none of the data, consumer profile, or experience, yet you know a thousand times more than these "geniuses" who try to copy it. I am writing this book for the same reason I built an educational website—so that you can learn how to develop your own marketing and sales programs. I am just using MMC®'s Cash campaign as an example so that you can see how this entire system came together and is revolutionizing an entire industry to inspire you to do the same for your own product or service. This book is meant to educate and inspire you to bring value and innovation to the golf industry.

MMC®'s Cash campaign was never meant to be a business model; the marketing concept is to give a course a jump start by acquiring hundreds, if not thousands, of golfers at one time from untapped segments of the market and convert those new golfers into long-term loyal members. Sadly, after many course owners run the Cash campaign, they became addicted to the cash and forgot this campaign was designed as a mulligan (a do-over or a second chance) to rejuvenate a course's traffic, revenue, and membership base by balancing out their books, membership base and tee-sheet. In no way is it meant to become the price point of a course or the norm for the entire industry. The long-term strategy is to acquire a surplus of golfers, continue marketing, while gradually increasing the green fees and membership rates, as well as raising the perceived value of the course within the community.

Over the years, I have been concerned about how I would come across if I wrote articles or spoke out on this subject of how and why the industry is dying a slow death. I shied away from doing so until now, because I didn't want to appear as bitter for people plagiarizing my materials or as if I were just trying to bash my competition—neither of which is true in the least bit. This is in no way a condemnation of my competitors or those who have borrowed portions of our campaigns. I am just shining a light on the weeds that are choking the industry and preventing the golf industry from growing.

Competition has never hurt MMC®, because let's face it: there are approximately fifteen thousand golf courses in the United States alone and to date we have only worked with two hundred plus thus far. There is plenty of business to be earned by all legitimate marketing companies. I believe in competition, but I believe in competing with individuals or companies who compete on their own merits. I believe in competing in a way that is going to benefit the industry as a whole and will make all of us working in this industry stronger and wiser. Conmen, plagiarists, cherry pickers, and copycats don't make anything better or bring anything of value to the table; instead, they are destroying the industry by ruining golf-course businesses.

I know no one likes to hear the negatives about something they love as much as we all love the game of golf. The game has suffered enough blows over the past fifteen years, and the last thing I want to do is shine a light on the hidden sores. I fell in love with the game that morning in South Carolina about twenty-five years ago, and over the past decade, I have spent every day promoting the game, growing the game, and defending the game with dignity and integrity. One of the biggest draws for me to the game was that it embodies the same characteristic traits I do—honesty, integrity, and loyalty—and I hope by my shedding some light on some of the negatives of the business people will be motivated to remember the code of ethics that is synonymous with the game and apply it to their business practices as well as their personal lives. In short, let's stop talking the talk and start walking the walk.

The game doesn't need to change—99 percent of golfers don't need to change, and 99 percent of owners, managers, and pros don't need to change—but those who felt a little sting when reading this chapter may want to rethink their values, change their ways of doing business, and represent this game and industry with the dignity it deserves. In some, if not most, industries, lying, cheating, and stealing are tolerated, if not expected, but I expect a lot more from those of us in the golf industry. We must hold ourselves to a higher standard, or we will destroy the industry beyond repair.

I never bring up problems unless I have solutions. In the next and final chapter, I will provide a solution to grow any golf business as well as the industry beyond anyone's imagination—far better and greater than it ever was in the 1990s!

CHAPTER 8

THE SOLUTION: GROWING THE GAME (REALLY!)

I n 2016, an estimated thirty-five million Americans expressed interest in taking up the game. The data also shows about eighty million Americans buying within golf categories, for example, products, merchandise, magazines, and so on. There are approximately thirty million core and avid golfers in the United States (roughly 10 percent of the almost 323 million Americans). This means there is a market of almost forty million casual and nongolfers just waiting to be engaged. Everyone in the industry, with the exception of MMC®, is targeting the same 10 percent and has completely ignored the other 15 percent. The true growth of this game depends on player-development programs that target the casual and nongolfers.

Recently, one of the industry's go-to organizations published an article on their interpretation of a profile of golfers; their profile was rudimentary at best. In short, it was nowhere near a workable profile. To make matters even worse, they were profiling core and avid golfers—the same segments the industry has been targeting for more than a hundred years. The article reminded me of when I first started the learning process back in the late 1980s, but I give them credit for giving it the ole college try. The golf industry is at least thirty years behind on this subject and has only become aware of it because MMC® brought it to the forefront back in 2006 and has been hammering it into everyone's mind ever since.

There are approximately 15,000 golf courses in the United States, which means the average course should have an average of nineteen hundred golfers based on the number of golfers in the United States. If the average membership in the United States was only $50 a month, then every course theoretically should be grossing a minimum of $95,000 a month, $1.14 million a year in just membership dues alone, and at least another $50,000 in back-end revenue, bringing the average course that is just getting their market share and not growing their business outside of the segments that are already committed to the game to $1.74 million per year.

You have heard me say it, and I am saying it again: numbers don't lie. With numbers like these, every golf course in America should be making money hand over fist, so why aren't they? It's because they are still running marketing campaigns from the 1990s and marketing to the same segment of golfers as their competitors: the avid and core golfers. Most courses need far more uncommitted golfers as committed golfers to balance out the books and membership base as well as the tee-sheet. Owners should be thinking in terms of fifteen hundred to three thousand golfers with the emphasis on casual and nongolfers coming from the uncommitted segment(s). The uncommitted segments play far fewer rounds but spend drastically more per visit than the committed segments.

A golf course hosting twenty thousand rounds a year on average only has approximately 660 unique golfers (chapter 4) playing 80 percent or even as high as 100 percent of their rounds. Unfortunately, those rounds are being consumed by avid and core golfers. To be really successful in this business, you need the same number of rounds consumed by casual and nongolfers. This means you need around two thousand casual and nongolfers based on the data, which prove that as a group they golf only ten rounds each year. With this model, you would have approximately twenty-six hundred unique golfers playing a total of forty thousand rounds (in a thirty-week season), leaving at least twelve thousand rounds available for green-fee play. Now that you have twenty-six hundred bodies, you'll have far more guest green-fee play, F and B revenue, cart revenue, range revenue, outing revenue, banquet revenue, lessons, clinics, new memberships, and so on. Commonsense alone tells you having 2,600 golfers promote your course via word-of-mouth marketing is far better than 600 golfers; especially if those 600 golfers are core golfers trying to keep the course a secret so they can have the course all to themselves.

Why hasn't any person, company, or organization other than MMC® been able to grow golf courses' business?

Because

- it's not the price;
- it's not the product;
- it's the prospect!

Like it or not, there is a new norm for the golf industry. If you own or manage a golf course and you want to thrive in the golf business or, worst-case scenario, simply be financially solvent over the next ten years, you had better suspend your ego for a few minutes and read this chapter with an open mind. The golf industry has yet to see its hardest hit, but it is coming and coming real soon. I have been predicting trends in the health-club industry since the early 1980s and golf since the early 1990s. Each time I have been spot-on but not because I am a Nostradamus wannabe. What I am is a lifelong student of marketing, sales, psychology, economics, history, social sciences, and more specifically, professional golf-membership sales. Here is what the data shows.

First, you must accept the fact that the spending habits of everyday people drive the economy—spending habits of groups or segments, not individuals. Not everyone (as an individual) falls into this matrix, but as a group, people do predictable things at certain stages in their lives. If you want to know the year, you are most likely to die, just ask your insurance provider, and after he or she asks you a few lifestyle questions, he or she will be able to give you a very good guess. These demographic realities are all based on data that has been collected and analyzed over decades. Similar data is available for the economy; if you simply know where to look and, more importantly, know how to interpret the data, you can easily see the future as well.

There is an enormous amount of data available that tells us at what age (as a group) Americans are likely to do certain things, make major purchases, and make life-changing decisions. For example, on average we join the workforce at around twenty-two years old; we marry at an average age of twenty-six; we buy our first home at an average age of thirty-one; we buy a bigger house at an average age of thirty-nine; and we are in a position to have our greatest disposable income (what is referred to as our peak spending years) at an average age of forty-six, which is when we tend to buy luxury items—sports cars and boats—travel more frequently, and so on. We tend to continue this spending pattern up to the age of fifty-three, and after that, our spending habits start to drop off dramatically because we then start saving for our retirement. We typically enter retirement at age sixty-three, and once we retire, our spending comes to a grinding halt, other than for medical-related expenses. This is not a guess; this is a demographic fact. This data is all over the Internet and absolutely free; look it up.

The reason the United States experienced a great rush in the 1990s was because we were in the middle of the baby boomers' peak spending years, and the icing on the cake was the great Tiger Woods brought youth and excitement to the game. Baby boomers were the largest generation in the history of the United States up to that point, and that is why golf courses experienced massive growth, which inevitably sparked the growth in the construction of new golf courses. Because of the baby boomers entering their peak spending years, golf courses had a huge influx of golfers. During the 1990s, everyone and their brother were opening golf courses. This is exactly why the so-called experts are claiming we now have too much inventory and not enough golfers. This statement is absurd as well as ignorant. There are plenty of golfers out there; the challenge is that some course owners, managers, and pros are living in the past and are too stubborn or egotistical to accept reality and change with the times.

I am not trying to guess the future of the golf business; I am just stating the facts. In no way is this chapter meant as a warning of Armageddon. Quite the contrary, it is a road map to financial freedom. People always say that knowledge is power, but I disagree; many of us know what we should do but never do it. Case in point, we all know we should eat healthy, exercise, and get six to eight hours of uninterrupted sleep every night, but do we follow those simple steps to a healthier, longer, happier life? This is, of course, a rhetorical question because even though we all know we should do these things, most of us still don't. Instead, the saying should be, knowledge coupled with action is power.

The great news is that the millennial generation is bigger (by almost 15 percent) than the baby boomer generation, which means that about a decade from now (2017), things will be rockin' again, and everyone (even the uninformed) will be making a fortune in the golf industry. The tip for the future success of golf courses is demographics because the millennial generation is far more diverse than the baby boomers.

The business of owning and marketing a golf course has changed, and it will be a decade or more before the industry gets anywhere close to where it was in past decades. If you don't change your antiquated business model and rethink your inadequate marketing, your business will die with the baby boomers. Forget marketing concepts of the past because they won't work with millennials, and do not be conned (convinced) by the false narrative that the only way to engage millennials is via e-marketing, social media, or other platforms of digital marketing. Most millennials change their platforms year to year, jumping on the latest, coolest platform. Yes, a working knowledge of digital marketing is essential, but first, you must create a model that offers products and services specifically tailored to the buying patterns and spending habits of this generation (not generations of the past); then, and only then, can you decide on the best delivery system to get the message or offer out.

Social-media platforms are changing so fast. First, the hottest platform was FB, then Twitter, then Instagram, then Snapchat, and so on. Targeting millennials is far more difficult than starting an FB or Twitter account. Millennials jump platforms like avid golfers jump from course to course, looking for the deal of the day. About every two years, there is a new popular platform. The only way to get in the millennials' circle and follow their next step is to get them in your circle first, and they (as a group) will keep you informed of the new trends in social media.

Again, this lack of information is just one more example of everyone missing the boat. Owners, managers, pros, and salespeople buy into the BS that saturates the Internet about e-marketing. Social-media marketers want you to believe you need them or you'll never engage millennials. The fact is that millennials have to live somewhere, and there is no better media to engage them than a personalized piece of direct mail.

For some reason, the so-called experts out there think you must reinvent the wheel, just as many industry people think they need to reinvent the industry and the game, when that is the furthest thing from the truth. You do need to update and upgrade your golf facility over time, but the wheel is the wheel, just as golf is golf.

The other day, I was speaking with one of my sons (Chaz), who was totally immersed in his devices and gadgets. I asked him why he was using his computer and iPad at the same time. He replied, "Dad, one is for streaming video, and the other is for gaming." He then informed me that his sister (Azha) uses three devices at a single time not only for gaming and streaming but also for chatting. Millennials are the new generation of consumers. If you can get to just a few millennials and your message resonates with them, you may get lucky and have your message go viral. But you would be foolish to assume this will happen. You must be well versed in all media and platforms so that you're not just hoping for a successful campaign but planting the seeds to ensure a successful campaign.

The biggest reason course owners want to focus on social-media marketing is because in their minds it's a free form of advertising. Yes, social-media marketing is free on the surface, but only after you build your list of prospects by engaging the public and getting them to opt into your list. Your FB page can draw business but only relative to your likes, friends, visitors, views, and followers. People who are successful at marketing through social media have a list of followers, and those who don't have little to no chance of maximizing these platforms. Most businesses that have experienced great success using social media and e-marketing have been building their lists for years.

Growing a business or growing a golf course is about building prospect lists and generating leads. The more leads you generate, the more chances you have at making a new sale every day or growing your business and your golf career. Think of it as having more chances at bat: the more leads you have, the better your chances of getting a hit (locking up a new relationship). The more effort you exert in generating leads, the more likely it is you will consistently lock up a new relationship; it's a numbers game. Learn to use social-media marketing wisely, and grow your list just as you grow a business. Think of your list as a bank: as long as you are making deposits, you can make withdrawals. When the deposits stop, it won't be long until your withdrawals stop as well.

List maintenance is simply maintaining your golf prospect and client lists: keeping them updated and clean. This is a crucial part of golf marketing because your marketing efforts are going to rely on the quality of your list. When people think of lists, they normally think of e-mail lists, but in marketing you should have numerous lists—a snail-mail list, an e-mail list, a mobile list, and so on. You want to maintain these lists so that when you launch a marketing campaign, you will be engaging qualified targets. One of the most important things when it comes to e-mailing, especially if you are using a third-party vendor (server) or even your own IP address, is to make sure you are not flagged as a spammer. It is easy to become a spammer if you send out many e-mails to an old or expired list. Spammers are despised in the Internet world, and your business will be affected if you are labeled as one. It is OK to send out one, two, three, or even four unsolicited e-mails at a time, but when you start sending out more than a handful or so of e-mails at one time, you can get flagged by your ISP as a spammer.

A typical example of this is when you buy or rent a snail-mail list (postal), and some unethical list company tries to get you to buy or rent an accompanied e-mail list. The list provider may claim 70 percent of the records (street addresses) are accompanied by e-mails. If you opt to move forward, you are taking countless chances of getting fined each time you or someone else sends a bulk e-mail to those addresses; one chance is too risky. Put aside the fines and possible criminal charges; the best of the worst-case scenarios (which is absolutely devastating to your online presence) is you destroy your domain name and get blacklisted by your ISP as well as all the major search engines such as Google, Yahoo, and Bing.

Some people and companies out there will try to sell you anything just to make a buck, not caring about the damage it can do to your business. You get what you pay for in life. You might be able to save a couple of pennies today, but you'll pay beyond your imagination for the life of your business. Buying an e-mail list knowing all this is pure stupidity. Ignorance is not knowing; stupidity is knowing but doing it anyway.

So always keep your prospect lists and client lists as clean as possible. Update them, take out the old contacts, and make sure you don't have a bunch of bad e-mails. The same thing goes for your mobile list, your snail-mail list, and so on; you want to maintain them on a regular basis.

Another point on digital or e-marketing that needs to be touched on is SEO (search-engine optimization). Understanding SEO is extremely important to maintain an online presence. SEO is the system or strategy used on the Internet to get better rankings with search engines such as Google, Yahoo, and Bing. When a prospect searches online to get information about a golf course and you have worked on your SEO, your golf course will appear in one of the top-five results on the first page. The reason you will want this position on the page is because if your site shows up after page one of the search results, the number of golfers who will see your information will be few if any. There are basically ten spots on the first page, and you want to be number one if at all possible. The search results statistics change day to day, as do the percentages of views and clicks that you receive by being number one, two, three, four, five, and so on. But on average, you are going to get probably 50 percent or better of the clicks if you're number one, and after that the percentages will go down to as low as 3 percent on the first page.

But the most important thing for you to understand when it comes to SEO is that your goal is to be a top-ranked golf course within your keywords search. For example, if you are in Chicago and someone types in "golf courses in Chicago," you want to be ranked number one with the top search engines. You can accomplish this by adding back links, writing blogs, putting keywords on your website, getting involved with social media, buying a domain name with your town and product in the address—for example, chicagoabcgolf.com—since prospects are more than likely going to search for Chicago golf courses, and so on. These are all essential tools to help you get a better ranking with the major search engines. The key thing is to make sure you provide free education and information on your website. You must also make sure to have new content often to keep the search-engine crawlers coming back to your site. This is one of the reasons businesses and individuals load up on social media: they want more traffic to their websites so that they can get better rankings with the search engines.

There are numerous mistakes you can make when it comes to your search-engine results and I am speaking from experience. In 2012 and then again in 2014, I had to make a decision to change MMC®'s domain name, which killed our ranking and made us start over from scratch. I decided to move away from using our original domain—which I had started in 1999 and was organically ranked number one or two on Google for more than a decade. Of course, this was against the advice of our in-house SEO specialist. But the word consultant doesn't define MMC® as a company because we specialize in the design and implementation of marketing campaigns. Believe me, it was painful to see competitors who started their companies five or ten years after MMC® jump ahead of us in ranking overnight. But sometimes you have to make difficult decisions, and since I knew we were in the business for the long haul, I bit the bullet.

Even though most digital platforms do not produce a stunning ROI, the long-term branding of your course, name recognition, brand positioning in the marketplace, list building, and so on will pay dividends tenfold throughout your career. You can't major in minor things if you want enormous success. Big numbers are relative; the more contacts you make, the more people you'll help and the more money you'll earn. So you must turn over every rock, not just the easy ones, and if you can't afford to hire the experts in those specific fields, you must learn a little bit about all the resources available to get your name, product, or service out into the marketplace.

A major component of running a successful business is ABP (always be prospecting). I believe in guerrilla marketing. Advertising is paramount to success; the more you do of it, the more success you will experience. Do it all, and do it always. When it comes to marketing and prospecting, stay consistent with your message, and keep your name in front of your targets. Timing is everything, and this holds especially true in advertising. I do strongly believe social media and e-marketing will be mainstream tools for marketing to all generations in another decade, so you better start preparing now.

Many people in the golf industry still rely solely on the Field of Dreams fantasy. They believe if they build it, golfers will come. Well, this is not the case and hasn't been for more than ten years. You must be actively generating leads. More leads equate to more revenue, and more revenue equals financial success and security. Everyone is depending on you growing your golf course and your career: your family, your owner, your community, your employees, and so on. Everyone, either directly or indirectly, is depending on your ability to generate new leads and turn those leads into new committed golfers.

Research is the biggest and best investment a golf course can make. Start by knowing your competitors and where you stand in the marketplace. How does your golf course stack up to theirs—pricing, facilities, and so on? It doesn't matter whether it is a muni, nine-hole, or even just a driving range; if any golf business is capturing just one golf dollar, it is crucial you know how much and why. MMC® conducts an in-depth competitive overview on all our clients' properties to make sure we know exactly what is happening in the marketplace.

Get to know your audience and who qualifies as your audience— your targeted demographic. No one can afford to incur wasteful spending. You must take into consideration all aspects of your targets: lifestyles, spending habits, buying patterns, geographical demographics, incomes, and education levels, just touch the surface. Naïve marketers look primarily at income as being the qualifying factor for membership, but income alone can be very misleading. You probably have your own example of this. Have you ever tried to roll out your own campaign targeting an area labeled "affluent," thinking it was your audience, yet you received a dismal return on your investment? In some cases, enormous income masks enormous debt. Some of these targets with high incomes can't afford to pay attention, much less pay for golf memberships. You definitely don't want to be in the collection business. Your desired target is consumers with disposable income, not consumers drowning in debt. Profiling your target is an absolute must!

Create the message you want delivered through your marketing that resonates with golfers. Build the brand you want people to associate with your golf course. Develop these aspects of your brand and repeat them often. Keep your brand and message in the marketplace, employing all types of media and platforms to deliver your message. Use the same consistent message and slogan, but be aware of changing the offer and hook in your marketing campaigns. Never drop the ball when it comes to marketing and getting your message out. It has been proven time after time throughout history that the companies that continue to market their business even in difficult times tend to outperform those that don't ten to one when the economy gets better. No matter what always keep some kind of advertising budget no matter how small it may be. You can't harvest a crop if you didn't plant the seeds. A small harvest is better than no harvest.

Mastering all media is a must for efficient marketing. Today, everyone is looking for the cheapest delivery system available. Simply put, courses are confusing motion for momentum. All media have a place in marketing and should be maximized when relevant. Radio, television, newspapers, social media, and e-marketing, along with a host of other platforms available, are great support tools, but none are as powerful as profiled, personalized direct mail when it comes to getting your message to your prime targets. Your target market as a golf course is no more than a thirty-mile radius (in most cases, but of course there are exceptions to the rule) from its location, period; anything outside of that is wasteful spending.

The power of a personalized offer that is tangible cannot be underestimated. The immediate and residual measurable dividends produced from a properly executed direct-mail campaign are far superior to those from any other form of marketing. Eventually, you want your golf course's name in every qualified consumer's mind within your radius. Direct mail is the best delivery system to make that happen.

Think of radio, television, Internet, newspaper, social media, and most other media as a shotgun that fires a shell full of hundreds of small pellets that scatter as soon as they leave the barrel of the gun, hitting anything and everything. Now, imagine a highly qualified sniper, wielding a scoped precision rifle with a range of up to thirty miles, locking in on his target and squeezing the trigger. There is no wasted investment and definitely no unwanted collateral damage (undesirables). Simply put, all other media are like hunting with a shotgun, and direct mail is like hunting with a precision sniper rifle.

Establishing a good relationship with your target market is a very important element in positioning your brand and maintaining its desired reputation in the marketplace. When it comes to brand management, most golf courses are confused as to who is responsible for this position. In reality, every person involved with your course is responsible for your brand management. The marketer is responsible for how your brand is communicated and perceived within the marketplace, and your front-counter person has just as much responsibility because he or she is responsible for the intangible part of brand management, which is the first impression and customer service.

Customer care, starting with answering the phone properly through assisting golfers and prospects alike when they come into your pro shop, will contribute a lot in building the reputation and brand of your course. Customer care includes taking time to understand how the prospect and golfer feels when he or she comes to your course. Are guests being left alone to fend for themselves, or are they given guidance and good service so that they feel welcome as valued members or guests of the course?

To grow your business, you must first know your prospect's core emotional needs and then design your advertisement to target his or her emotions, not yours. Another great benefit of brand management through superb customer service is that birds of a feather flock together. If your golfer is a core or avid golfer and financially qualified to buy a membership, preferred-players' card, or annual pass, then the odds are good that his or her friends are as well. If you capture one golfer and get him or her committed to a membership or loyalty program, then when it comes time for his or her buddies to choose a golfing home, they will definitely choose your golf course because their buddy is already in a committed relationship with the business.

So far, I have given you all of the components you need to launch any product or service in the market. You have learned the importance of research and data; I have provided you with the most in-depth sales system known to man; I have taught you a dozen low to no cost ways to generate business; I have taught you how to successfully market your product or service; I have taught you everything you need to know to successfully grow your business. Now I am going to teach you how to put everything together piece by piece. The best way for me to do this is by using my own product as the example. I am going to show you how I built MMC®'s Cash campaign and how I market it so you can use it as an example for your **own** product or service.

When designing a new product or selling an existing product, you must ask yourself a million questions, and the first three of those questions must be, who is my customer, what are my customers' biggest headaches, and how can my product eliminate them? For MMC® our customers are owners of golf courses, managers, and golf pros. The six big headaches for our customers are loss of rounds (revenue), most owners have no money for advertising or are unwilling to invest into advertising because nothing they have ever done has ever produced worthwhile results, unmotivated or unqualified staff, no innovative ideas or out-the-box thinking to grow the business, no time to make a change, and fear of things getting worse.

When designing my product, I addressed and eliminated the headaches of golf course owners because I designed the Cash campaign to specifically address owners' headaches all the while showing how my campaign will eliminate all their problems, and I started with the big one first; our campaigns require no up-front fees or out-of-pocket expenses! Then I moved on to the others: the introductory membership sells itself making the sales process as easy as order taking so that there is no need to hire or worry if the existing staff can handle the sales; the campaign is innovative and new to the industry because we penetrate untapped segments of the market, our staff does 99 percent of the work behind the scenes to prevent overload and the course's staff feeling overwhelmed, which also makes the campaign worry free, leaving the owner with the only thing to fear, is fear itself.

By mastering all media and platforms, MMC®'s team has developed, tested, and successfully implemented a customer-building approach that is unprecedented in the industry today. Specifically, we are able to address the stagnant marketplace by tapping into new segments, therefore generating immediate cash, monthly receivables, member retention, and revenue growth for golf courses. This is no longer a theory but a proven method, and it's a powerful solution for our participating golf courses.

Our approach involves a loyalty-based relationship that will connect with your market. Today's courses are faced with at-risk memberships, green fees, F and B revenue, merchandise revenue, outing income, and so on, which has been attributed to the current economic climate, lifestyles, and conditioned spending habits of today's golfer. With so many places to golf available, customers are leaving their home courses for discount and bargain green fees. Our research has shown that this group accounts for an average of one-thousand golfers within many markets with a population of twenty-five thousand households or more. Unfortunately, these golfers and their rounds are being divided up by multiple golf courses. Marketing to these golfers with coupons, daily deals, and so on only conditions them to wait for the next deal to come along, whether it's from you or your competitor. You can't build long-term relationships and member loyalty in a four-hour round. Relationships require repetition; just like building a muscle, they don't take shape overnight.

MMC®'s model is designed to bring golfers in on an introductory membership and lock up the long-term relationship (retention is built in) from the beginning. This model gives the course's staff ample time to cultivate the new relationship as opposed to the one-round or ten-round deals that dilute the message of golfer loyalty. I understand these short-term deals are presented by the vendors as "loss-leaders" to get golfers through the door to give the sales staff an opportunity to sell them a membership, and if the staff are well trained, not lazy, don't take shortcuts, follow a professionally designed sales presentation, and the golfer is qualified, this marketing concept can be effective. My pushback is that there are too many ifs.

The MMC® approach offers a no-risk, self-funding solution to execute market-dominating campaigns to grow your loyal customer base. The program start-up requires no cash outlay on the owner's end; MMC® is paid only on performance, and the course owner will handle (and deposit into his or her bank) all the funds generated. The program is truly no-risk and self-funding and, therefore, self-propelling. Each phase of the campaign, from the start and moving forward, is propelled and funded by the previous phase. If for any reason the revenue to advance the campaign has not been generated by the campaign, the owner may cancel our agreement at any time without any further financial obligation to MMC®.

MMC® works on a success-only basis, so we receive absolutely no payment unless we are successfully growing your business. MMC® provides the demographic research, market analysis, campaign design and implementation, sales training, coaching, materials, extensive support, consumer profiles, ad copy, ad design, ad layout, and project manager to guide you effortlessly through every stage of the campaign, eliminating any guesswork and wasteful spending and, therefore, delivering the desired result: a successful no-risk, self-funding golfer-acquisition marketing campaign targeting casual and nongolfers, which starts growing your business today!

Each project has a unique personality and is custom-designed to meet the needs of the owner or operator. However, it is MMC®'s responsibility to provide a balanced perspective, ensuring that each campaign connects with the local market in a way that can achieve the final goals of the business: to connect with the casual and nongolfer, engage millennials, rebuild loyalty (as it was in the 1990s), develop unmatched player retention, eliminate discounting green fees and memberships, capture higher dollars per round, and build a sustainable business model for the life of your business.

Since 2006, over 90 percent of our partnering golf courses have raised more than $100,000 in immediate cash with many of those properties raising as much as $500,000, all in ninety days or less with our no-risk self-funding Cash campaign. So when we make the claim that we are the world's leader in golf marketing, we have the track record to prove it.

Having a great golf course to offer your customers is only part of the big picture. Times have changed, and knowing what to do and what not to do is the difference between a campaign that raises $30,000 with no residual income and a marketing campaign that raises $300,000 with increases in back-end revenue by as much as 500 percent. The up-front number (cash collected at the point of sale) is directly proportionate to the residual income you can expect to see from just two of your profit centers: cart fees and food-and-beverage. Getting golfers and prospects through the door is the challenge of today's owners and operators. Furthermore, getting these golfers to commit to your golf course as their exclusive course of choice is an even bigger challenge.

Most marketers are oblivious to or lack the resources to important components of a successful marketing campaign such as demographic research, market analysis, consumer profiling, professional sales training, data on consumers' buying habits and spending patterns, and so on. It takes in-depth knowledge of all these areas to maximize your marketing dollars for the greatest ROI while preventing wasteful spending. MMC® knows the power of personalization and has invested in a full-time, twenty-four-hours-a-day, seven-days-a-week research-and-development department that devotes 100 percent of their time to profiling your ideal golfer. These efforts have produced an unparalleled formula for success by utilizing a variety of campaigns for raising immediate cash and monthly receivables, increasing daily traffic, and planting the seeds for long-term residual income through increased player development and player retention around the country. MMC® leaves no stone unturned when it comes to growing your business, and the best part is MMC®'s programs are 100 percent no-risk and self-funding!

MMC® has three programs for helping owners and their businesses achieve long-term financial freedom:

1. The Cash campaign
2. The EFT (electronic funds transfer) campaign
3. The Elite campaign

MMC® also custom-designs six minicampaigns (absolutely free) for our clients to run internally after running MMC®'s Cash campaign. These minicampaigns are designed specifically to capitalize on the increased traffic generated by the Cash campaign and maximize the earning potential of the course's profit centers. By launching these minicampaigns, our clients will begin to condition their golfers' spending habits.

Giving freebies and bonuses is an incredibly valuable tool in building long-term relationships, so invest in caps, logo balls, logo shirts, and towels, and start giving out freebies. I practice what I preach, so I have built in numerous added benefits and freebies such as the six minicampaigns for the golf courses that chose to partner with MMC®.

MMC®'s three campaigns are scheduled to be launched every year in a specific chronological order, one right after the other, so you'll want to save some of the cash from the initial Cash campaign to fund the second two campaigns. MMC®'s Cash campaign will bring in $100,000–$500,000 in immediate cash at the point of sale, as well as hundreds or thousands of new golfers. This will be your foundation to start building on. During this first year, you will not have the time to launch any of the minicampaigns, nor will you need to. Your primary focus must be on customer service.

The following year, you will want to launch MMC®'s EFT campaign, which will offer a significantly more expensive membership than the introductory membership offered in the Cash campaign. This campaign will focus on raising the perceived value of your course within the marketplace as well as increasing your monthly receivables. The EFT campaign will bring in fewer golfers than the Cash campaign, so don't expect as huge an influx of golfers during the second year as you had with the Cash campaign. You will start seeing a slight drop-off in rounds this year, so you will want to compensate for the attrition by running the EFT campaign. The attrition rate will be determined by your previous year's customer service, so do not let up on customer-care programs. This second year, you will launch one or two of the internal low- to no-cost minicampaigns to increase revenue in one or two of your profit centers.

The third year, you will launch the Elite campaign, targeting a more affluent demographic with a much higher price point and again increasing the perceived value of your membership within your market. You will also launch one to two more minicampaigns for one or two more profit centers. The Elite campaign will bring in far fewer golfers than the Cash and EFT campaigns but will cost far less since this demographic is much smaller. MMC®'s Elite campaign is designed for increasing the value of the course's brand as well as acquiring new golfers. This campaign is not a huge moneymaker but will pay for itself tenfold.

Here is what I mean: After the third year, the introductory memberships will be coming up for renewal. If you have done everything right and the economy hasn't gotten worse, you can raise your membership rates and green fees even more until you reach a fair market value because you have been slowly increasing the course's perceived value within the marketplace over the past two to three years. If for some reason the economic climate hasn't changed, you can launch another Cash campaign, raise the price point of the introductory membership, and start the cycle over but with an increased perceived value within the marketplace. You will never offer the original price point again because you never want the market to perceive you as a $100, $200, or even $300 course. You want to be perceived as a course of value and great customer service where your golfers get results and build lasting relationships, not just one that offers cheap membership.

Marketing requires thinking outside the box. One technique employed by MMC® is to design golf-course memberships with a low barrier to entry as a hook (the draw) for grabbing the attention of casual and nongolfers, but price can never be your only point of leverage, nor can it ever be presented as the superior part of your golf product or services. It can be used only as a hook to get prospects' attention. This is where most owners and operators sink the ship when trying to implement this kind of campaign on their own. All they see is the tip of the iceberg—the initial offer (the hook)—but they fail to see the enormous substance supporting the tip from beneath.

Even when this marketing hook is deployed by MMC®, there is no danger of engaging the undesirable consumer, thanks to MMC®'s vetting system for qualifying prospects. There is also a built-in foolproof safeguard to eliminate any undesirables from buying a golf membership: the course's staff collect all membership revenue and signs all membership agreements. In short, the final decision to approve the applicant or not is yours; you maintain full control.

The worst thing you can do is take this price point and run it year after year or, just as bad, run it on a very limited basis and not maximize its potential. It's like giving a patient the prescribed dosage of a medicine. Too much will result in an overdose, and not enough is just as bad as not doing anything at all. The proper dosage is required if you want the patient to overcome the illness. Once you've made the decision, don't try to put the medicine back in the bottle. Go for it; there's no reason for you to stop and pull back. Just enjoy the ride and build on the momentum. Do not use MMC®'s marketing concept as a business model; use it as a tool.

This exciting new membership program will substantially enhance your ability to provide current golfers with an even greater value than ever before. This program involves a very aggressive membership-growth initiative. It is important to note that this new program offers a membership opportunity far different from anything you have provided in the past and, as such, is not directly comparable to the membership plans to which you are accustomed. We believe you will be incredibly excited about this one-time offer, as this new membership category is specifically designed for the casual and nongolfers in your community and will provide the greatest value your course will ever offer. However, there are dramatic differences between your premium (platinum) membership and this introductory membership, so there is no reason to worry your existing golfers may migrate to the introductory membership offer.

MMC®'s Cash campaign is designed to be launched in four phases:

We start with a soft internal launch with signs around the property and e-mails to present and past golfers. The revenue collected from this soft launch is then used to seed the direct-mail campaign. During this time, MMC®'s staff will be pulling all the demographic data, compiling it for the profiling process, studying the competitive overview, creating ad copy and design, training your staff, and so on in preparation for the external launch.

The second phase is some local newspaper and radio ads. Although these media are dying, they still have some listeners and readers who are core and avid golfers. A campaign like ours is based on guerrilla marketing, and you must not leave any stone unturned. These delivery systems are especially important for getting the word-of-mouth marketing started.

The third phase is the driving force of the campaign: direct mail will be deployed through four consecutive mail drops to profiled targets selected on a criteria-based formula. This is the most important phase of the campaign. This entire campaign has been designed around targeting the casual and nongolfer to balance out the tee-sheet while increasing revenue through all profit centers. If you are not 100 percent committed to this phase of the campaign, do not embark on this campaign because you will just deplete your core customers and ruin your business. The success of this phase is based on the profile. If you do not have access to the profile and have the proper tools to engage casual and nongolfers, do not attempt to run (ruin) this campaign. Each week's direct-mail launch is determined and propelled by the previous week's intake of revenue. So at no time is the owner at risk or out of pocket to fund the direct mail.

MMC® has had courses stopping the Cash campaign after bringing in five hundred golfers or so only to regret their decision of not going deeper into the campaign within just a few short months. Stopping early is a huge mistake; you'll never get another chance to build off the momentum once it is gone. MMC®'s Cash campaign is designed to bring in the masses, and it only makes sense when targeting casual and nongolfers and the goal is volume from the beginning. Then and only then will the business have the surplus of golfers necessary to raise membership rates or green fees without worrying about the attrition rate.

The fourth and final phase of our Cash campaign is the closeout. This is when all media and platforms are enlisted. We leave no stone unturned. You can easily raise 20 percent of the total gross of the campaign in the last two weeks when the closeout is managed properly. Again, the campaign is set up this way with built-in adjusters to accommodate the circumstances. If the client has reached the desired results before the closeout, the client can choose to do a soft, quiet closeout; if the client is short of the desired result, the client can choose to push the closeout as hard as necessary to achieve the desired result. Either way, the closeout is extremely important because not only do you lock up all the last-minute procrastinators, but you also inform the community that this once-in-a-lifetime opportunity is coming to a close and will never be offered again. This announcement helps you get back to your original pricing. In addition, it gives you a "real" reason why you can no longer offer the introductory membership since you are under contractual agreement with a company, whose offices are based in Jacksonville, Florida, that specializes in growing the game, and they are the ones in charge of this campaign. You can honestly say your rates have always been X, and this was just a campaign designed and managed by MMC® to bring community awareness to the game of golf.

The next step is forward thinking. Now that the owner has raised some cash, paid the bills, and put some money in the bank and a little in his or her pocket, he or she can start preparing for the future growth of the business with MMC®'s EFT campaign.

Our EFT or monthly receivables campaign is designed to raise our clients' monthly receivables. After closing out MMC®'s Cash campaign, our clients are not looking to raise quick cash since they ran our Cash campaign the previous year, but they would love to add to their current membership base. This EFT campaign is designed exactly for that. Instead of advertising a PIF (paid-in-full) membership, we offer an introductory membership on a monthly payment model, although we can incorporate a PIF option for those courses that wish to raise a little more cash as well. MMC® has also designed a three-tier membership for our EFT campaign, just as we have for our Cash campaign. It is extremely important to stay consistent with your marketing message and model. During the second year, the course should launch one or two more of the minicampaigns as well.

The following year, the course should launch MMC®'s Elite campaign. This campaign targets an affluent demographic with disposable income through demographic profiling and select consumer spending. MMC®'s staff will consult with you and custom-design a marketing campaign around your current business model, membership rates, and budget. This campaign is designed to attract consumers where cost and inconvenience can be overcome by the prestige of belonging to and having the best. Because there are far fewer consumers who fall into this category, you can expect to have far fewer prospects; all things are relative. This platinum membership is the full all-inclusive membership you may currently have in place today. MMC®'s team will just dress it up and make it more attractive, more desirable, and, therefore, more sellable. During the third year, the course should also launch one or two more of the minicampaigns as well.

Courses should always start with the Cash campaign to balance out the tee-sheet and raise revenue, even if cash is not an issue. All golf courses have debt that needs to be paid or equipment leases that can be paid off to ease the financial burden that is hindering the business's growth. Besides, you'll need cash to support the other two campaigns. Every business should have at least a five-year marketing plan to guarantee the growth of the course, and this is why I have structured this model to grow any course for a minimum of five years. Every golf course should have at least six different marketing campaigns designed and ready to launch at any time. With six campaigns, you will have your marketing strategy prepared for at least the next two to three years.

With just a little bit of thought, it is easy to take the same old products or services and spin them in a different light. As a marketer, you must have a strategy and always be ready to launch a campaign in a moment's notice. Be creative. You do not have to change your business; all you have to do is make it more appealing to more people. Since I started working as a consultant in the mid-1980s, it has been challenging to get owners and managers to commit to a marketing strategy that will carry them throughout the year, much less over the next five years. Ninety percent of the time, they are so happy with the cash collected that they forget about the pain that got them to call MMC® in the first place.

MMC®'s Cash campaign's supremacy over any campaign ever designed for the golf industry goes unchallenged. Most courses—and marketing companies, for that matter—would never be able to afford, have the resources, or have the personnel to launch this mammoth campaign. Never in most courses' histories or futures would they have the opportunity to knock on every casual and nongolfers' door in their immediate areas and deliver their courses' message completely uninterrupted. MMC® has made it possible because our campaigns completely pay for themselves, and our team performs 99 percent of the work behind the scenes; that is why I say MMC® is golf marketing on steroids. Our clients' golf courses' membership gets bigger, and the course's financial health gets stronger within just ninety days.

The Cash campaign was never meant to be a business model; it is simply meant to be a marketing campaign that takes a course through the difficult times or slow seasons and positions the business in the marketplace where the owner can engage and acquire more golfers at a much higher price point in the future. In most cases, if you can capture the largest part of the market or dominate your market the first time, then you can go right back to your original rack-rate membership and green fees immediately, and you won't need to run the Cash campaign ever again. Once you have established your rates and your perceived value within your community, you can do smaller-scale campaigns to sustain the growth you've already achieved.

Always guard against the downside. The only possible downside to MMC®'s Cash campaign would be inexperience, incompetence, or laziness. The campaign can't fail; only the human components can. This is not the type of campaign you let an amateur hack at to see whether he or she can get the campaign close to the pin or inside the leather. These innovative golf-marketing campaigns require a team of marketing professionals who are up to par with relevant data and have experience in growing businesses. There is a bright future for the industry. My five-year plan is a sustainable business model for the long-term growth of any golf course.

MMC®'s Cash campaign is for every golf course in the world, not just struggling properties. It is everyone's responsibility in the golf industry to grow this game and introduce it to everyone. The first step is engaging the casual and nongolfers. As I stated earlier, there are fifty million Americans who have made purchases within golf categories, showing an interest in the game. These consumers are the untapped market for golf courses. If there are approximately fifteen thousand golf courses servicing only thirty million golfers out of the possible eighty million consumers with an interest in golf in the United States today, that leaves a possible growth of almost 200 percent for every golf course in business. If you are considering building a golf course but have hesitated because of the false narrative that the industry has been overbuilt, there is too much inventory, or the supply is outpacing the demand…break ground today—the numbers don't lie. Golf is the greatest game in the world, and I want to share it with each of the fifty million consumers who have yet to swing a club.

The lower "lost-leader" marketing concept is a win-win; it is a hook for businesses to grab the attention of consumers who have not been properly engaged. This introductory membership allows the new golfer limited access and all other products and services are à la carte. Golf courses are a business and must be profitable to motivate owners to stay in business. These introductory golfers pay lower membership fees, and for getting such a great value, they agree to play during the course's slow times of the day and slow seasons. They choose to adjust their schedules accordingly and have the option to stay in the introductory membership category or upgrade to a full-course membership, either at the point of sale or anytime during the term of their membership. They pay extra for any additional products or services they choose to buy.

With this membership category, golf is affordable for all Americans and profitable for all course owners. Owners are filling in dead times of the day with golfers who will spend in the profit centers, and the consumers get a great introductory rate. This concept will not be successful if it is targeting the core and avid golfer. This campaign is designed specifically for the untapped segments of the market, and MMC® is the only company with the proprietary right to the formula. There is an old Chinese saying that goes something like this: "If you handle a master carpenter's tools, be prepare to hurt yourself."

Touching people's lives in a positive way has been extremely rewarding for me over the years. Exercise, proper eating habits, and plenty of uninterrupted sleep are the triad to a long, happy, healthy life. MMC®'s Cash, EFT, and Elite campaigns are the triad for the financial health of a golf course. I am so proud and grateful I was able to help millions of people enjoy the game of golf and help owners thrive in this business. I fell in love with the game that summer day in South Carolina, and I hope by reading this book you will have a renewed love for the game and business as well.

Wishing you good health and prosperity,
Chuck Thompson

PS: Please take a few minutes to write a review for my book, and post it on as many websites and platforms as possible including Amazon with a direct link to where your friends and followers can buy Golf: The Untapped Market—Why the Pros Are Failing to Grow the Game. Also, be sure to register with my company and personal websites—www.mmc today.com, www.golfmarketingmmc.com, and www.chuckthompson. guru (not dot com)—for freebies and updates. If you wish to contact us at MMC®, you may call 904-217-3762, call toll free 877-620-8135, or e-mail me at chuck@mmctoday.com. For comments or any other correspondence, please use my personal address at chuck@chuckthompson. guru (not dot com).

Thank you.

Mulligan:

A mulligan is when a golfer or business gets a second chance to take another shot, whether it's a shot at a pin to improve the golfer's score or a golf course getting another shot at growing its business with no penalty—a do-over. (Chuck Thompson)

MMC® has a mulligan for growing your business today.

Mulligan Marketing Concepts® Since 1991

Made in the USA
Columbia, SC
09 December 2017